HOW IT WORKS

in the City

ALLAN PUBLISHERS, INC.

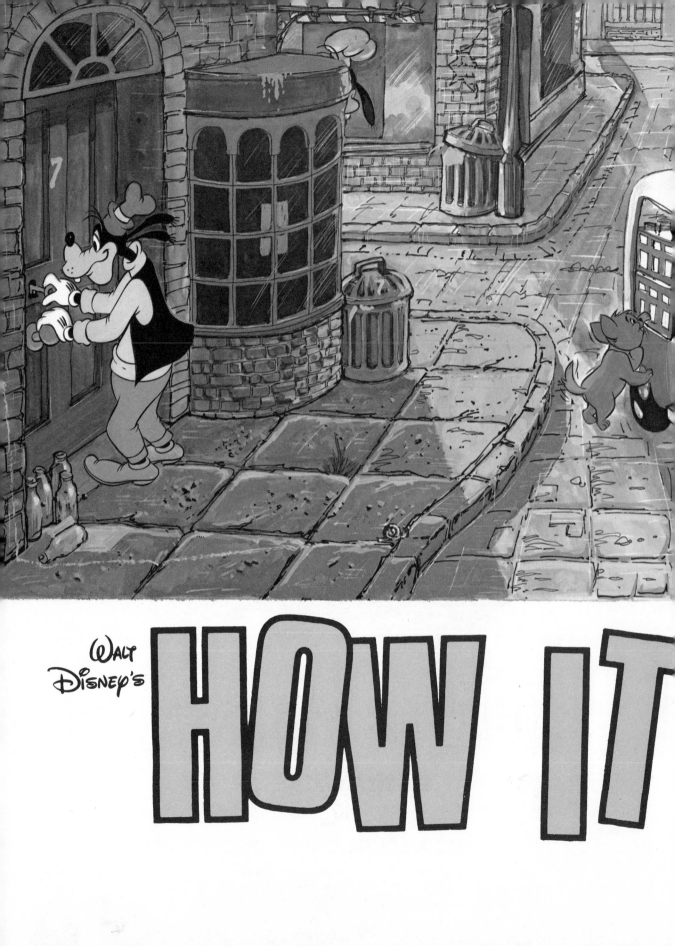

WALT DISNEY's HOW IT

WORKS
in the City

Contents

Introduction

The first cities grew up when Man gave up hunting to become a farmer. That was about 10,000 years ago; but until about 200 years ago most people still lived in the countryside. Then came the Industrial Revolution, and people began to flock into the towns and cities.

Today in North America, Western Europe and other parts of the world, something like three-quarters of the population are city-dwellers. The human race has become urbanized. "Urban" means "of the city."

Some of the biggest cities, like Tokyo

and London, have a population of ten million people or more. In addition to the people who live actually in the cities, millions more travel to and from the cities each day to work. They form the huge commuter population.

The cities are centers for shopping, numerous trades and businesses, travel, tourism and entertainment and therefore have to provide the necessary facilities – good shops, plenty of office space, reliable public transport, ample car parking space, railway stations, airports, theaters, movies and so on. To cope with these demands the cities have had to grow both in size and complexity. This book will give you a glimpse of the varied activities that take place in the city and help unravel some of the city's mysteries.

On the Streets

The streets of the city throb with life throughout the day, as shoppers bustle to and fro and workers go about their business. Along the main streets of the city center are situated the large department stores, which sell all kinds of goods – books and buttons, food and fridges, hats and hardware, television and toys. There, also, are the large chain stores and supermarkets, where service is "help yourself." In between are the smaller shops which sell a smaller range of goods, but give you personal service. With so much to spend your money on, it is fortunate that the banks are close by! Fortunately, too, there are plenty of restaurants and cafés to pop into when you feel hungry, as you will at the end of a morning's shopping.

9

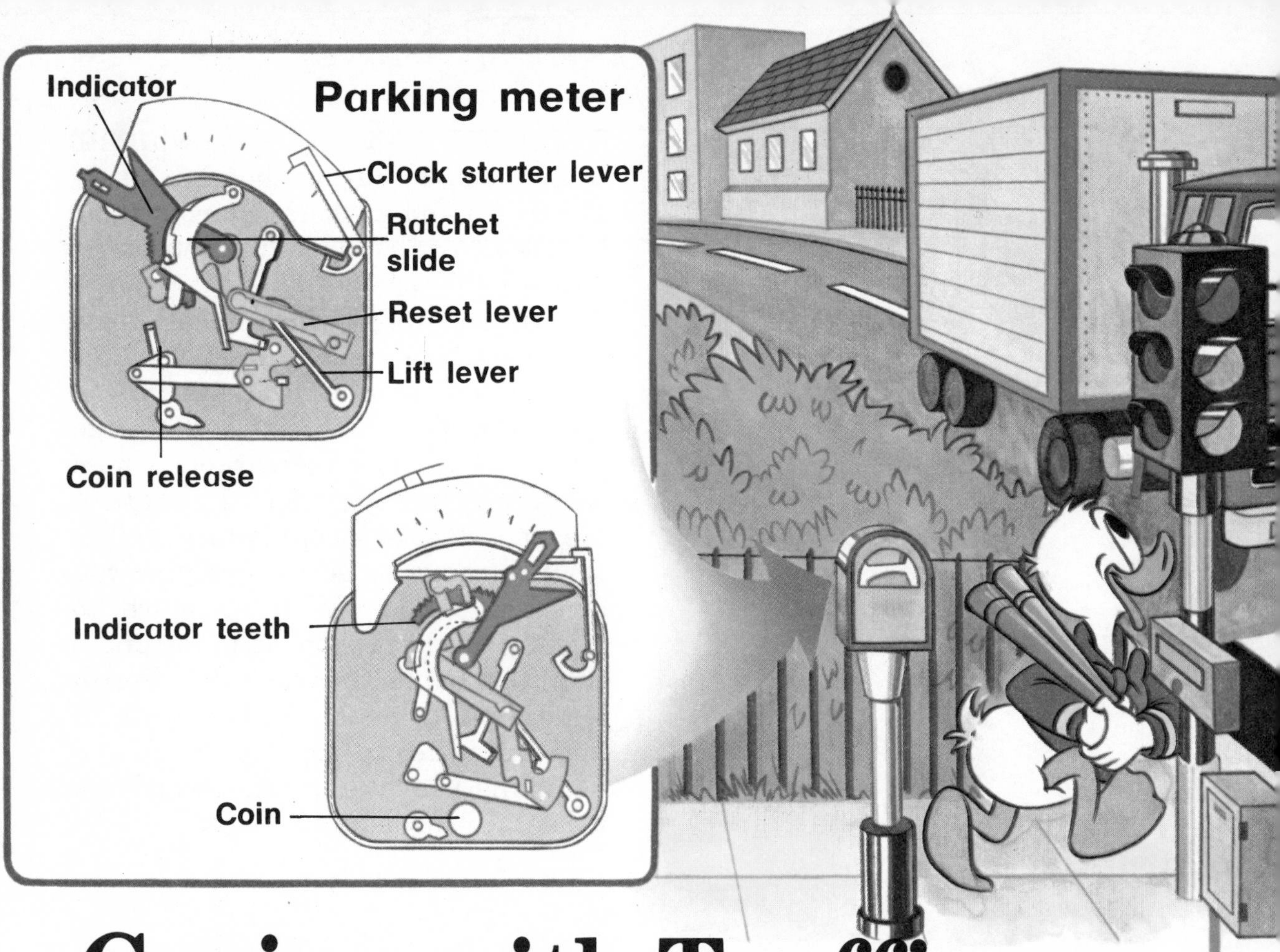

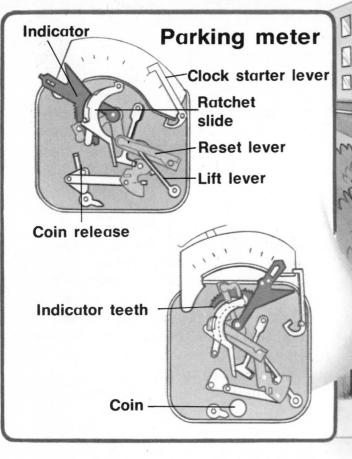

Parking meter

Indicator

Clock starter lever

Ratchet slide

Reset lever

Lift lever

Coin release

Indicator teeth

Coin

Coping with Traffic

These days the city is full of traffic, and you must take very great care when crossing the road. Wherever possible, cross where there is a pedestrian crossing or a traffic light.

Most traffic lights work automatically. They generally have sets of three lights – red, amber, and green, facing in different directions: toward the main street and a side street at right-angles to it. The lights facing each street show different colors to stop traffic going along one street and allowing it to go along the other.

The lights show red to make the traffic stop and green to let it go. The amber light by itself means "caution." The sequence of light changes is: red; green; amber; red.

This sequence continues endlessly, worked by automatic switches in the traffic light control box. The switching mechanism is shown on the right. It is controlled by a rotating camshaft. As the camshaft turns, the cams close or open the switch contacts to switch the appropriate lights on or off.

The movement of the camshaft itself is controlled by a timing device, the timer drum, which rotates at constant speed. On it are several raised keys. As they turn around, they close a pair of contacts. This switches on an electric motor that makes the camshaft turn.

In many cities finding a place to park can be a problem. Sometimes you can

Traffic lights

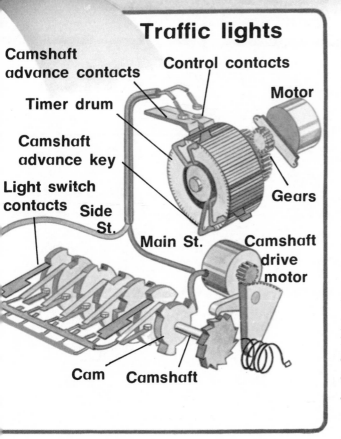

Camshaft
advance contacts

Control contacts

Motor

Timer drum

Camshaft
advance key

Gears

Light switch
contacts   Side
            St.

Main St.

Camshaft
drive
motor

Cam   Camshaft

park free of charge in side streets away from the shopping center, but usually you have to pay. The parking lot may be in the open air or in a special building, a parking garage, see page 14. Or you may be able to park on the street at a coin-operated parking meter.

The meter contains a clock device, which has to be wound up, usually weekly. When a coin is inserted in the meter, it trips a series of levers which start a timer. They also move an indicator over a scale marked in hours and minutes. This tells you how much parking time you have bought. Some meters operate only with one type of coin. Others operate with different coins, each one buying a different amount of parking time.

The city streets are busy not only on the surface but also underneath. If you had X-ray eyes, you could see all kinds of things buried beneath the road and pavements. In some cities, you might even find railroads and rivers running there!

In any city you will find a multitude of cables, pipes and channels beneath

Out of Sight

the streets. These carry the services that a modern city cannot do without. For example, there are often several pipes carrying fresh water – the water

Pavement

Road

Curb

Drain

Manhole

Cable duct

Electricity cables

Water main

Telephone cables

Inspection chamber   Maintenance engineer

Main sewer

Out of Mind

mains. From these mains branch off smaller pipes carrying water to the buildings along the street.

At intervals along the pipes there are valves, or stopcocks, which can be closed to cut off the water when, for example, a leak occurs. They are reached from the surface through small shafts, or open vertical pipes. There are also tap-off points, or hydrants, here and there, from which water can be piped from the mains. Firemen use them, for example, when they need water to fight fires.

Other pipes and channels carry dirty water beneath the streets. Rain water from the surface runs into the gutter because the road is cambered, or raised slightly in the middle. It flows into so-called storm drains and from these into a much larger channel called the sewer. The storm sewer may also carry waste water from the buildings, but often this is discharged into a separate sewer and flows to a sewage treatment plant outside the city. Some sewers are large enough for people to walk through.

Gas mains, electricity cables and telephone wires also thread their way beneath the streets. The gas mains are usually made of cast iron or plastic and like the electricity cables are simply buried in the soil. The more delicate telephone wires, however, are threaded through ducts, or conduits, usually made of earthenware pipes. At intervals the ducts are led into a large inspection chamber, containing junction boxes. It is reached through a manhole on the pavement.

So much goes on beneath the streets that any road repairs and excavations must be carried out with great care. Otherwise the city could end up without water, gas, electricity or telephone services—and what chaos that would cause!

Telephone booth

Gas main

Water hydrant

Telephone cables

By-pass valve

Gas supply pipe

High-rise Parking

To ease traffic congestion in the streets, many cities now provide off-street parking. The parking lots may either be in the open air or under cover in a many-level, or multi-story building. In most lots you have to pay to leave your car.

At some lots you simply pay an attendant as you enter. At others you buy a ticket from a slot machine, which you then stick on your car's windshield. The ticket allows you to park for only a certain time, so the machine stamps on it the time of issue.

In other parking lots you are automatically issued with a ticket as you enter, as in the multi-story garage illustrated here. Blocking the entrance to the car park is a barrier. In front of it is a ticket dispenser which you can reach through the car window. When you stop by it, a detector loop beneath the road surface sends signals to the ticket dispenser that a car is present, and the dispenser automatically issues a time-stamped ticket. Once you have taken the ticket, the dispenser sends signals to the barrier in front of you, which then lifts up. Another detector loop senses when you have driven past the barrier and sends signals to lower it again.

When you want to leave this car park, you present your ticket to the attendant in the exit booth. He notes what time you entered the park and charges you for the time your car has spent there. He then presses a button to raise the exit barrier. This lowers automatically as your car passes over another detector loop.

Control box

Driving sheave

Governor

Suspension cables

Guide rails

Counterweight guide rails

Counterweight

Inspection pit

Buffers

Passenger elevator

Most multi-story parking garages have an elevator to carry drivers to and from the floor on which they have parked. The elevator moves up and down between guide rails. It is supported and hauled by a cable that runs up and over a pulley system, or sheave, at the top of the elevator shaft. The sheave is driven around by an electric motor at a constant speed, controlled by a governor. At the other end of the suspension cable is a counterweight which helps balance the weight of the passengers and makes it move more easily.

Multi-story car park

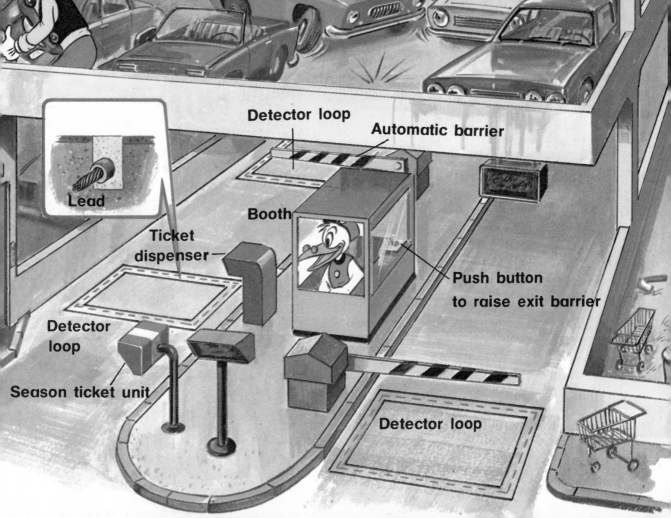

Lead

Detector loop

Automatic barrier

Booth

Ticket dispenser

Push button to raise exit barrier

Detector loop

Season ticket unit

Detector loop

Pointer

Weight scale

Sliding weight

Pendulum

Scale

The Personal Touch

In modern cities many of the shops are of enormous size. There are huge supermarkets, for example, which sell food and often many other things besides. At these stores all the goods are on display for you to see. All the goods are marked with their prices. When you want something, you simply take it down from the shelf.

Some shoppers, however, prefer the friendly atmosphere of the small family shop. They like to chat with the owners and the people who serve them and catch up with gossip. Foods like cheese and cooked meats are freshly cut for you, and not prepacked as they are in supermarkets. The shopkeeper weighs them on old-fashioned scales,

Coffee grinder

Lid

Glass hopper

Stopper

Removable container

Spiral grinder

Electric motor

Main knife edge

Pan

Knife edges

Counting arm

Adding wheels

Cam

Cam

Type transfer wheel

Cash register

Indicator

Keybar

Segment

Block

Swivel arm

dulum and pointer. The pendulum acts as a counterweight to the object in the pan. The lever moves the pointer across the scale to show the weight of the object. The weight range of the scales can be adjusted by altering the position of the sliding weight.

The shopkeeper keeps the cash he takes in a cash register, or till. In a simple, keytype register he just presses down the appropriate keys to record the total cost of your shopping. The amount appears in the window of the register. As he presses the keys, a drawer opens in which he puts the money. The register also has a device that prints out the amount of money "rung up" on the keys. This helps the shopkeeper to keep his accounts straight.

The simple cash register works mechanically. Others work by electric-

perhaps like the one shown here.

On this scale the object to be weighed is placed on the pan. The front of the pan dips and pulls down a rod which lowers one arm of a lever. Attached to the other arm of the lever is a pen-

ity and also act as adding machines to add up the cost of different items. The one shown here has an electric motor which turns a series of arms, wheels and cams to work the adding, display and printing mechanisms.

The Department Store

The small family shop often sells only one kind of thing, such as food or clothing. In contrast the big city store sells all manner of things, from hats to hi-fis, pens to pajamas, tiepins to television sets, succulent steaks to silk stockings. It is many shops rolled into one. It is called a department store because it is made up of separate departments on several floors.

Usually there is a manager in charge of each department and often a "floorwalker," who is in charge of the salespeople. Also mingling with the crowd of shoppers are several store detectives. Their main job is to catch shoplifters – people who pick up goods when they think no one is looking and leave the store without paying. In many stores now the detectives and security chiefs use closed-circuit television to help them keep an eye on what is happening in the store. They watch TV screens, or monitors, which receive pictures from TV cameras dotted around the various departments.

The larger stores have electric elevators or escalators, as well as stairs to take shoppers from floor to floor. The elevators may be worked by attendants or they may be automatic, being worked by the passengers themselves. The main doors of the store may also

Closed-circuit television

Monitor

Coaxial cable

Lens

Camera

Power Cable

Floorwalker

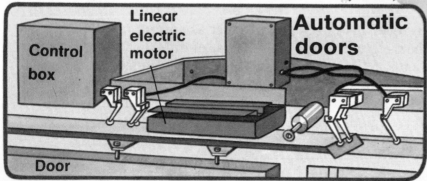

Linear electric motor

Automatic doors

Control box

Door

operate automatically so that they open before you reach them. They may be worked by pressure pads beneath the floor, which send signals to the controls box when you step on them. The control box then switches on an electric motor which pulls the doors open. The doors close when the pressure on the pads is released. Other automatic doors are worked by invisible waves beamed out on either side of the opening. When someone or something approaches, the waves are reflected back, and this triggers the control unit into opening the door.

Tag tape spool

Return spring

Figure setting knobs

Rubber pad

Ink pad

Handle

Printed tags

Printing roller

Pulling up the handle presses the tape against the inked figures. Releasing it pushes out the tape and the pad reinks the roller.

Price tag printer

Cash register

Bank On It

With so many tempting goods in the shops, it is just as well that there are plenty of banks in the same area. When you run short of money during a shopping spree, you can write out a check and exchange it for cash at the bank.

Most people now keep their money in a personal bank account. They pay their wages into the account, and pay their bills with checks drawn on their account. In this way they do not have to carry so much money about with them, or keep so much money at home. Under the mattress was always a favorite hiding place, as every burglar used to know!

At the bank, however, your money is safe. It is locked away in reinforced vaults, or strongrooms, and only a few people know how to unlock them. The vaults have complicated combination locks which can be opened only by someone who knows the correct combination. This is a series of numbers which tell you how to turn the dial so many times to the right, then to the left, alternately several times. There may be a million or more possible combinations to a lock, which makes it very difficult to "pick," or open.

Many bank vault locks have a further means of protection. They are time locks, which can be opened only at certain times of the day. At other times they will remain closed, even if the right combination is dialed.

The vaults and other parts of the bank are also protected by several burglar alarms which ring bells outside the bank and in the local police

Bank vault

Combination lock

Electric beam

Security system plans

CENS

station if they are set off by intruders. The alarms may be triggered off when the intruders break electrical circuits or step on pressure pads beneath the floor. They may also be set off by "magic eye," or photocell devices. These work when someone steps through a beam of light or invisible rays. Closed-circuit television may also be installed at the bank.

As you can see, as well as keeping your money secure, the bank must keep their security systems top secret to keep burglars away from people's money!

Time lock

Burglars

Alarm pressure pad

The Telephone Exchange

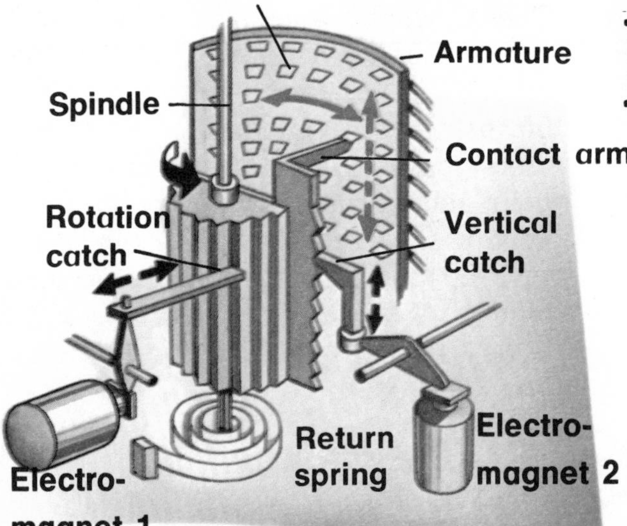

Contacts

Armature

Spindle

Contact arm

Rotation catch

Vertical catch

Return spring

Electro-magnet 2

Electro-magnet 1

Dialing the number

When you make a telephone call, lots of things happen "behind the scenes" to make sure you are connected to the correct number. Wherever you are, your telephone is connected to a telephone exchange.

In a manual exchange the operator works at a switchboard. This has sockets called jacks connected to all the telephone lines. To connect you to the

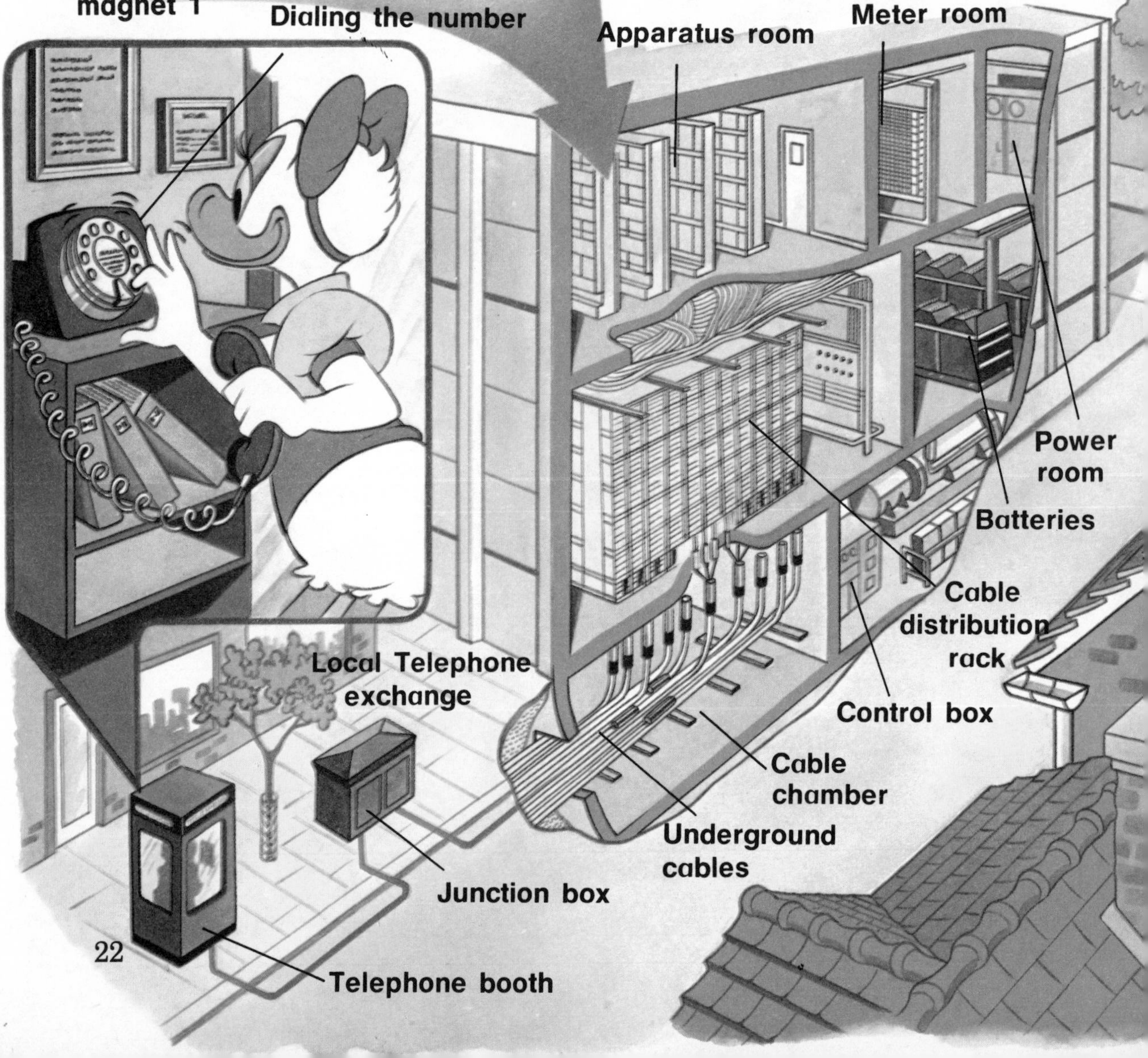

Apparatus room

Meter room

Power room

Batteries

Cable distribution rack

Control box

Cable chamber

Underground cables

Local Telephone exchange

Junction box

Telephone booth

person you want to talk to, the operator puts connecting plugs into your jack and that of the person you are calling. In an automatic exchange the operator's help is not often required. You make your own connections by dialing.

When you dial a number, your tele-

a simple three-figure exchange. As you dial "8," eight electrical pulses go to electromagnet 1 of the first selector switch. Each pulse causes it to pull the armature, which makes the catch raise the contact arm one level, so "8" will make the arm rise to level eight. Electromagnet 2 then moves the contact

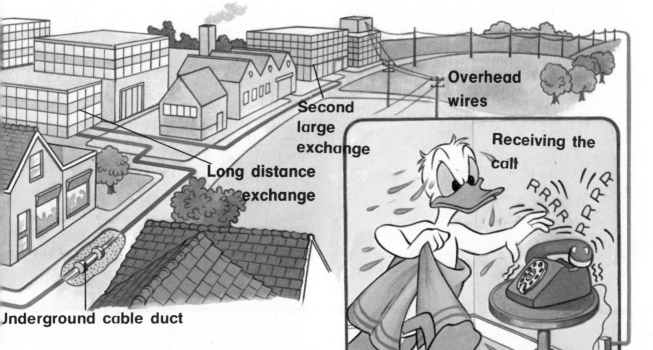

Second large exchange

Long distance exchange

Overhead wires

Receiving the call

Underground cable duct

phone sends tiny pulses of electricity down the cables leading to the exchange. For example, if you dial 3, three pulses will be sent, and so on. The pulses work switching apparatus at the exchange. In some exchanges the switching is now being done electronically by means of circuits like those in your radio and television sets.

In others it is still done by means of relays, which are switches worked by electromagnets. An electromagnet is a coil of wire which becomes a magnet when electricity passes through it. The picture at the top of page 22 shows one common type of relay selector switch.

Suppose you dial the number 863 on

arm around until it finds a contact which is not being used.

Your call then passes to a second selector. As you dial "6," the six pulses cause the contact arm in the second selector to rise to level six. When you dial "3," the three pulses make electromagnet 2 move the contact arm round to the third contact, which is connected to the line you want. Another relay then sends pulses down that line to ring the bell of the telephone of the person you are calling.

Space Age Telephoning

Today you can not only telephone people anywhere in your own country, you can also telephone people in other parts of the world.

Today most calls go by way of communications satellites. These satellites are stationed 22,300 miles (35,900 km) above the Earth on the Equator. To give the greatest coverage, the satellites are placed over the Atlantic, Pacific and Indian Oceans.

Suppose you want to make an overseas call. You phone through to your local exchange, which then connects you with the international exchange. The operator there then dials and makes the necessary connections to

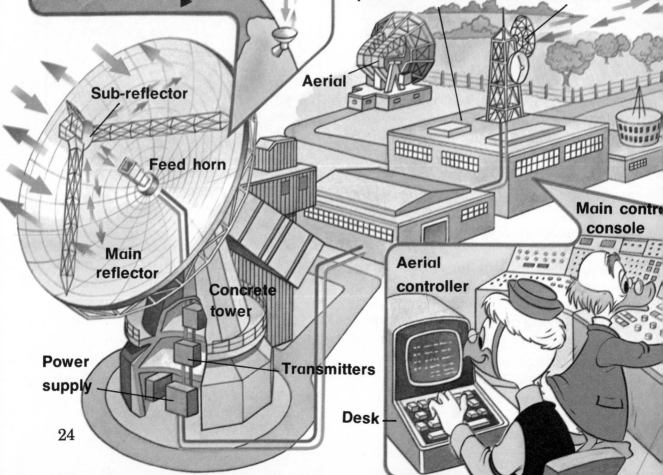

Satellite relays signals between ground stations

Solar panels

Overseas aerial

22,300 miles

Sub-reflector

Feed horn

Main reflector

Concrete tower

Power supply

Transmitters

Operation control area

Microwave tower

Aerial

Main control console

Aerial controller

Desk

route your call overseas. The signals the operator sends go to a satellite ground station.

If this is a long way away, the signals are first changed into microwaves (kinds of radio waves), and sent through the air rather than through cables. They are passed on by a series of microwave relay towers, spaced at intervals along the route. The towers contain equipment which receives, strengthens and then retransmits the signals.

Eventually the signals reach the satellite station. There they are again strengthened before being fed to the transmitting aerial, or antenna.

The signals go to a feed horn in the

Transmit and receive tower

Receive path

Repeater station

Transmit path

International exchange

Local exchange operator

Switchboard

Jacks

middle of the aerial dish, and are directed at a small reflector positioned above it. This reflects the signals on to the main reflector, which then sends a parallel beam towards the distant satellite.

The satellite receives the signals, which are now very weak, so it strengthens them and beams them down to another ground station. The receiving station collects them in another huge dish aerial, strengthens them again, and feeds them into the telephone network. This will carry them by way of relay towers and exchanges to the line of the person you wish to call.

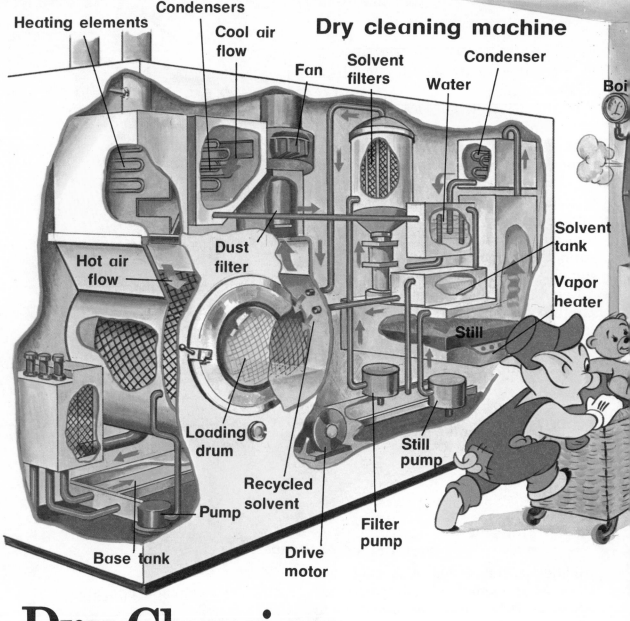

Dry cleaning machine

Heating elements

Condensers

Cool air flow

Fan

Solvent filters

Water

Condenser

Boi

Solvent tank

Vapor heater

Still

Dust filter

Hot air flow

Loading drum

Still pump

Recycled solvent

Filter pump

Pump

Drive motor

Base tank

Dry Cleaning

Many of the clothes we wear can be cleaned simply by washing, including sweaters, socks, shirts and so on; but other clothes, such as coats and suits, would be ruined by washing. They would lose their shape and smart appearance. This is because soapy water gets right into the fibers of the cloth and makes them swell and change their shape. For these kinds of

clothes, the answer is dry cleaning.

The term "dry cleaning" is rather misleading because a liquid is used in the process. A better term would be "chemical cleaning." One of several chemicals may be used in dry cleaning. Two common ones are called perchloro-ethylene and white spirit. White spirit is the same liquid that painters use to thin paints. These liquids are known as

Pressure
adjustment
wheel

Head

Feed
pipe

Buck

Operating
pedals

Steam press

solvents because they dissolve the grease that holds dirt on to clothes.

The kind of machine dry cleaners use to clean clothes is shown here.

The clothes are put into the loading drum, and then the solvent is added. The drum turns around, and the tumbling action helps shake the dirt loose from the fabric. After a while the dirty solvent is removed, and fresh solvent is added to rinse away any remaining dirt. Next the solvent is again removed and the drum is rotated rapidly to "spin dry" the clothes. Finally hot air is blown through the clothes to dry them thoroughly.

The rest of the equipment in the machine is designed to prepare the solvent for re-use. It includes a still,

which purifies the dirty solvent, and a filter to remove any dirt and fluff.

In the still a heater makes the solvent boil. The vapor coming from it is pure. The dirt remains behind. The vapor rises into a condenser, where it is cooled by coils of cold water. When it cools, it changes back into liquid and goes into the solvent tank. From there it is pumped back to be used again.

The clothes come from the dry-cleaning machine rather crumpled, and so they have to be pressed back into shape. This is often done by a steam press. Steam is used to apply both heat and pressure to the clothes. The operator works the press by means of foot pedals.

In the Office

In recent years the skyline of most of our cities has changed a great deal. Once the highest buildings were the churches, now the skyline is dominated by massive, skyscraper office buildings.

Every kind of business needs an office of some kind, whether it produces drawing pens or steel girders. The office is needed to deal with the paper work – letters to customers and suppliers, sales invoices and receipts, accounts, memos to other branches, and so on. Also, as every businessman will tell you, the amount of paperwork grows each year!

Fortunately, machines are on hand to help them cope with the problem. Most widely used is the typewriter, which has been with us now for over a hundred years.

Touch Typing

The most familiar sound in any office is the clatter of typewriter keys. Some typewriters are noisier than others. Some of the older mechanical typewriters sound like a machine gun firing, while the latest electric typewriters pitter-patter like falling raindrops.

Important parts of a typewriter are the keyboard, ribbon and the carriage. The carriage carries a rubber-faced cylinder, around which the typing paper is wrapped. When you press a key on the keyboard, a series of levers makes a bar carrying a piece of type come up and hit the paper. Between the key and the paper, however, is an inked ribbon, and where it strikes, the key prints a letter on the paper.

When the key is released, the type bar falls back into place. Also, the carriage moves along one space, ready

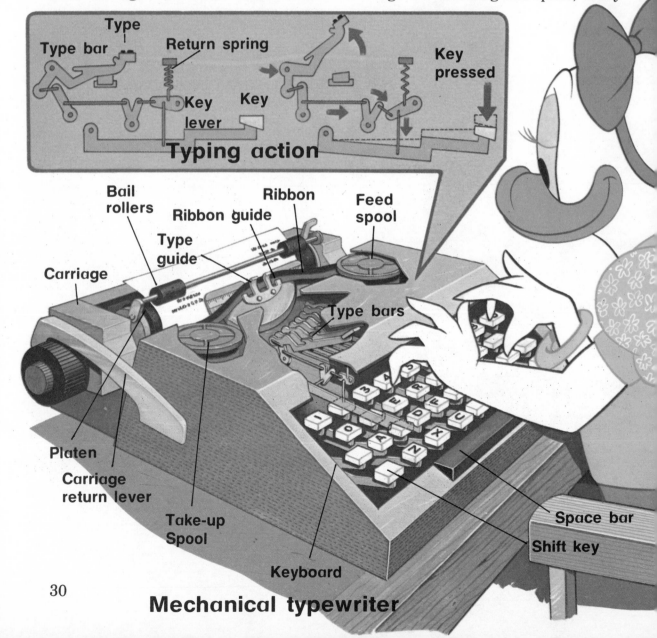

Typing action

Mechanical typewriter

for the next letter to be typed. At the end of a line, you move the carriage return lever to the right. This does two things. First, it turns the cylinder and paper around so that the keys will strike a new line. Second, it moves the carriage in position for the start of the new line.

There are two pieces of type on each type bar. One gives the letters of the alphabet in small letters, like this. The other gives the letters in capitals, LIKE THIS. You can type in capitals by first pressing a shift key. This moves the whole key assembly so that the capital letter type strikes the ribbon. The other main control on the typewriter is the space bar. You press this when you want a space between the letters you type, as between words.

The electric typewriter is mechanically similar to the ordinary typewriter except that it uses electric power to move the type bars. When you press a key, a raised cam moves into contact with a rotating roller. The roller carries it along a short way, and this movement in turn moves the type bar.

An interesting kind of electric typewriter has a different kind of typing mechanism. It has a ball-shaped typing head, and is often called a "golf ball" typewriter. The head is covered with rows of type, and is rotated and tilted to bring the right piece of type into position.

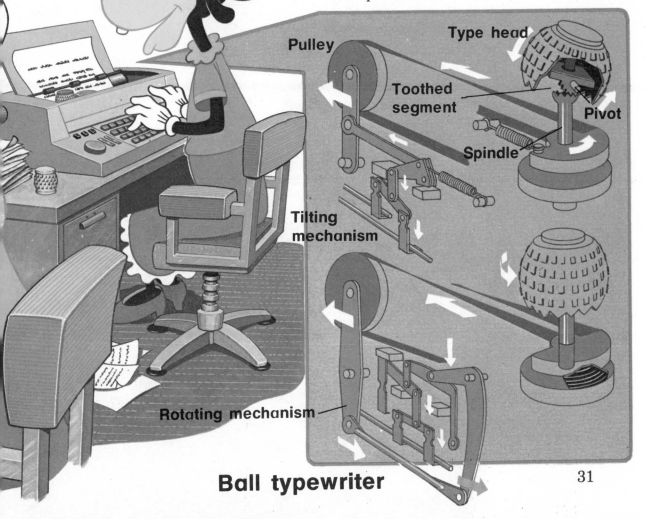

Ball typewriter

31

Copycat

Often in an office people need to make copies of letters or bills. If a typist wants 2 copies of a letter, she uses carbon paper. She places the carbon paper between two sheets of ordinary paper and feeds it into her typewriter. When the typewriter keys hit the top copy, they press a coating on the back of the carbon paper on to the sheet of paper beneath it to form an image.

To make copies of other things, she must use a copying machine. Most machines use a kind of photographic method.

One is called a wet copier because a liquid is used to prepare the copy. The item to be copied is placed on top of a sheet of special paper and exposed to the light of a lamp. An invisible image is transferred to the paper. This is then passed through a liquid, which develops, or brings out the image. The developer changes the invisible image into a visible one to make the copy. Some copiers use ammonia fumes rather than liquid to develop the image.

The other, dry copier, uses heat to develop the image. Two kinds of special paper are needed. The document to be copied is placed face down on the first paper (negative) and exposed to bright light. Then the second paper (positive) is placed on top of the negative, and the two are fed past a heater. The heat brings out an image on the positive paper.

One of the first dry copiers was the Xerox machine ("xerography" means "dry writing"). The dry copier is also called an electrostatic machine because it uses electric charges to form the image.

Receiving tray

Developer indicator

Front cover

Main switc

In such a copier, the document is exposed to strong light. A moving mirror reflects an image of the typewriting on the document, via another fixed mirror on to a rotating drum. The drum is coated with a metal called selenium and given an electric charge by an electrode. Where light strikes the drum, the charge goes away, but it remains where the drum is dark—where the image of the type is.

Electrically charged powder (toner) is then sprinkled over the drum and sticks to the charged (type) areas on the drum. The copy paper too is charged. When it is rolled against the drum, the powder is transferred to it. The coated paper then passes through a pair of heated (fusing) rollers, and the powder forms a permanent image.

Wet copier

Exposure control dial

Pressure plate

Paper-feed table

Guide plate

Reload lamp

Fixed mirror

Selenium-coated drum

Original document

Exposure box

Developer mechanism

Hood

Lens

Copy paper

Copy output

Oscillating mirror

Fusing rollers

High-voltage electrode

Dry copier

Office Supplies

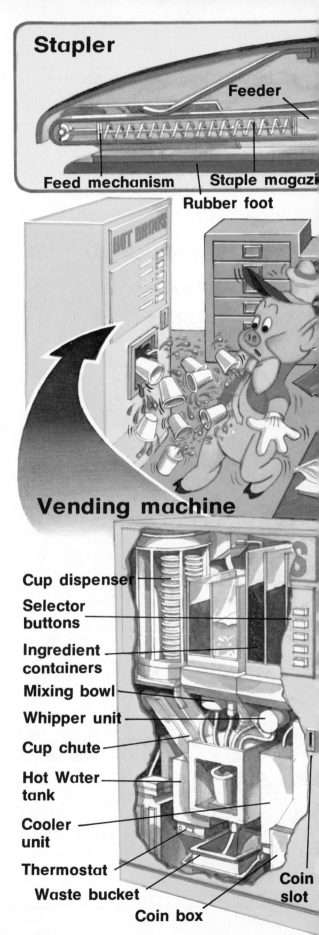

Stapler

Feeder

Feed mechanism

Staple magazi...

Rubber foot

Vending machine

Cup dispenser

Selector buttons

Ingredient containers

Mixing bowl

Whipper unit

Cup chute

Hot Water tank

Cooler unit

Thermostat

Waste bucket

Coin box

Coin slot

Many other machines and devices, large and small, assist you in the office. To join together the many bits of paper you deal with, you need a stapler. When you press the handle of the stapler, a blade pushes out a steel staple. It passes through the paper and strikes the anvil. This has grooves in it which bend over the ends of the staple to prevent the paper slipping off.

A pencil sharpener is also a handy thing to have. The one shown here has rotating cutters turned by cogwheels from a handle.

You will also need space in the office for filing, or storing the papers you want to keep. If you don't have a good filing system, you may take hours to find the letters and documents you need. The best method is to use a filing cabinet. This has drawers which glide easily in and out on runners and rollers.

The best way of fitting the papers into the drawers is by suspension files. These are files which have metal bars at the sides. The ends of the bars project and rest (are suspended) on bars on either side of the drawer.

When you are trying to put your papers in order, your work can be ruined if someone leaves the door open and a draft blows in, so it is a good idea to have a door stop. When the door is

34

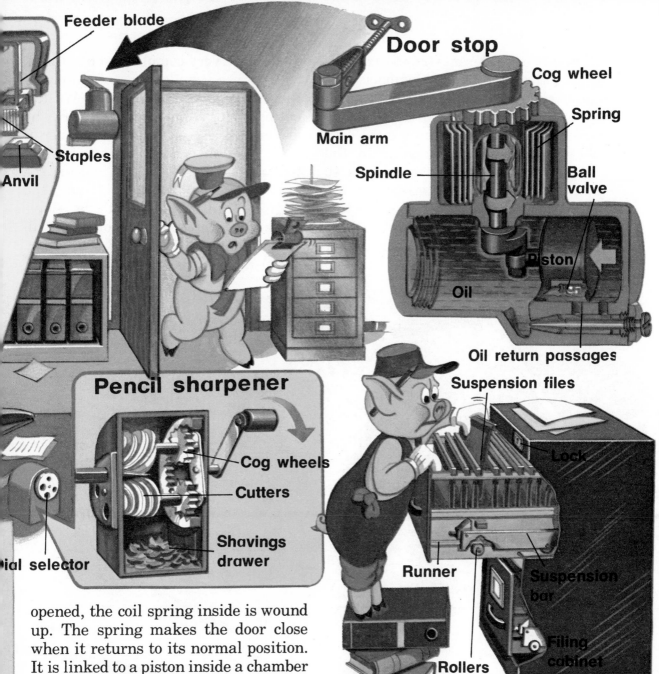

Feeder blade

Anvil

Staples

Door stop

Main arm

Cog wheel

Spring

Spindle

Ball valve

Piston

Oil

Oil return passages

Pencil sharpener

Cog wheels

Cutters

Shavings drawer

ial selector

Suspension files

Lock

Suspension bar

Runner

Rollers

Filing cabinet

opened, the coil spring inside is wound up. The spring makes the door close when it returns to its normal position. It is linked to a piston inside a chamber containing oil so that it doesn't move back too quickly.

From time to time during our working day, we all need to take a break for a cup of tea or coffee.

We can have a simple coffee or tea maker, or we can have the kind of machine shown here, which can serve, or dispense, a variety of different drinks. They include coffee, tea, hot chocolate and soup. We can have our

drinks with or without sugar and with or without milk.

To get a drink, you put in a coin and press the selector button for the type of drink you want. A paper cup slides down the chute beneath the outlet points. The appropriate ingredients are mixed with water, and pour into the cup.

Cars of many different shapes and sizes throng the city streets. Compact cars, convertible sports cars and huge, expensive limousines are all to be found there, and sometimes even very old, "veteran" cars as well. In the morning and evening rush hours so many cars take to the streets at the same time that traffic often grinds to a halt. It is usually quicker at these times to travel on a motorcycle, or motorbike.

Cars are very complicated machines, which are made up of literally thousands of different parts. We can better understand how a car works by grouping these parts into a number of basic systems. Each system has an important part to play in making the car go. Such systems include the engine, transmission, braking, steering and suspension. Each of these will be considered separately.

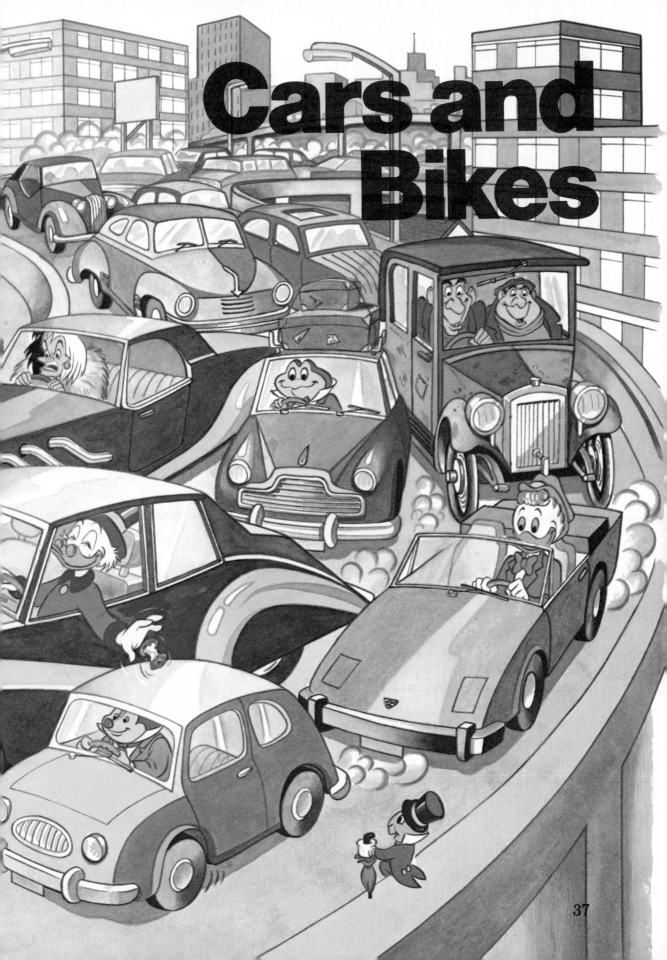

Cars and Bikes

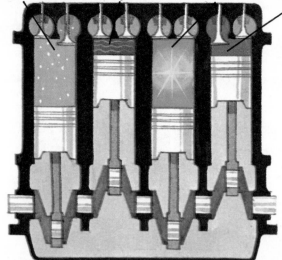

1 Intake   2 Compression   3 Power   4 Exhaust

Hollows in the head form the top of the cylinders. The head carries valves to let gases go into and out of the cylinders. It also carries the plugs which make the sparks that burn the fuel.

Both the cylinder block and cylinder head have passages running through them. It is through these passages that water circulates to keep the engine cool. Motorbike engines are different because they are cooled by air (see page 58).

Not all car gas engines are the same.

The Engine

The engine is the part which provides the power to turn the car's wheels. In the engine, fuel is burned to produce hot gases. The hot gases push against pistons, which move up and down inside cylinders. The pistons turn the shafts that connect with the car's driving wheels. Because the fuel is burned inside closed cylinders, the engine is called an internal combustion ("inside-burning") engine. Most car engines use gasoline as fuel.

We can think of the engine, too, as being made up of different systems. One system provides the fuel. One supplies a spark to burn the fuel. One keeps the moving parts oiled, while another keeps the engine cool.

The main body, or block of the engine, is usually made out of cast iron. It is put together in three main parts. One is the cylinder block, which contains the cylinders. Beneath the cylinder block is bolted a tank, or sump, to carry the engine oil. On top of the cylinder block is the cylinder head.

Hot water

Cooling fan

Radiator

Cooling air

Many cars have engines which contain four cylinders arranged in a line. It is this kind of engine that we show in the illustrations appearing on this and on the following pages. Other engines may have six or more cylinders, arranged either in one line, or in two lines, making the shape of a V.

Engines differ greatly in their power, which is usually given as so many horsepower. ("Horsepower" is a power unit originally based upon the average rate of working of a horse.) The engine of a compact car might produce about 50 horsepower while a sports car might produce over 100 horsepower.

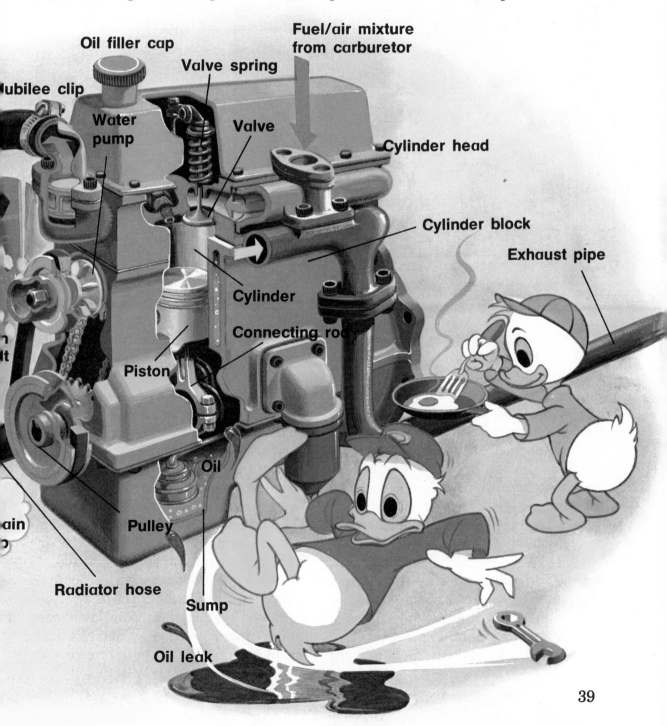

Oil filler cap

Valve spring

Fuel/air mixture from carburetor

Jubilee clip

Water pump

Valve

Cylinder head

Cylinder block

Exhaust pipe

Cylinder

Connecting rod

Piston

Oil

Pulley

ain

Radiator hose

Sump

Oil leak

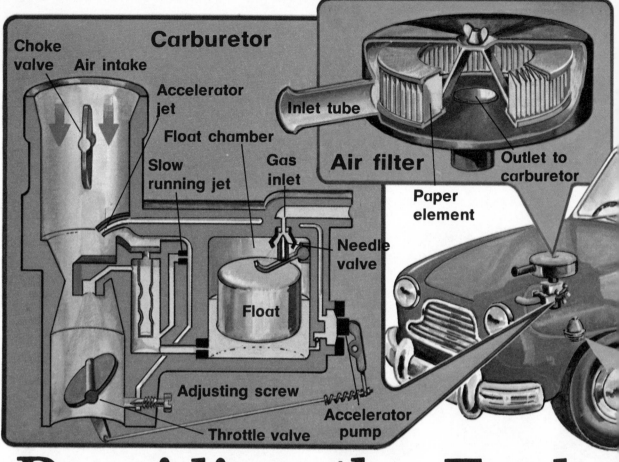

Carburetor

Choke valve

Air intake

Accelerator jet

Float chamber

Slow running jet

Gas inlet

Needle valve

Float

Adjusting screw

Throttle valve

Accelerator pump

Inlet tube

Air filter

Paper element

Outlet to carburetor

Providing the Fuel

A car stores the gas it needs in a fuel tank. In the usual kind of car with a front engine, the fuel tank is placed at the rear. It is always placed as far away from the engine as possible so that it does not become overheated. If this happened, it might explode, because gas is highly inflammable. From the fuel tank, the gas is pumped into the engine by a fuel pump.

The fuel pump shown here works mechanically. It has a lever which is rocked back and forth by a raised shaft, or cam, driven around by the engine. Movement of the lever pushes a disc, or diaphragm, up and down. On each downward movement, gas is sucked in from the tank, and on each upward

movement it is pumped through to the engine. Other fuel pumps work electrically.

The gas enters the engine through a carburetor. This is a device which mixes the gas with the air it needs to burn inside the engine cylinders. The air enters the carburetor through an air filter, usually made out of paper. The filter removes any dust in the air. The gas enters the carburetor through a float chamber. This controls the gas flow by means of a float valve. It contains a hollow float which floats in gas. When the chamber is full, the float rises and pushes against a lever that shuts a "needle" valve. When gas flows out of the chamber into the carburetor

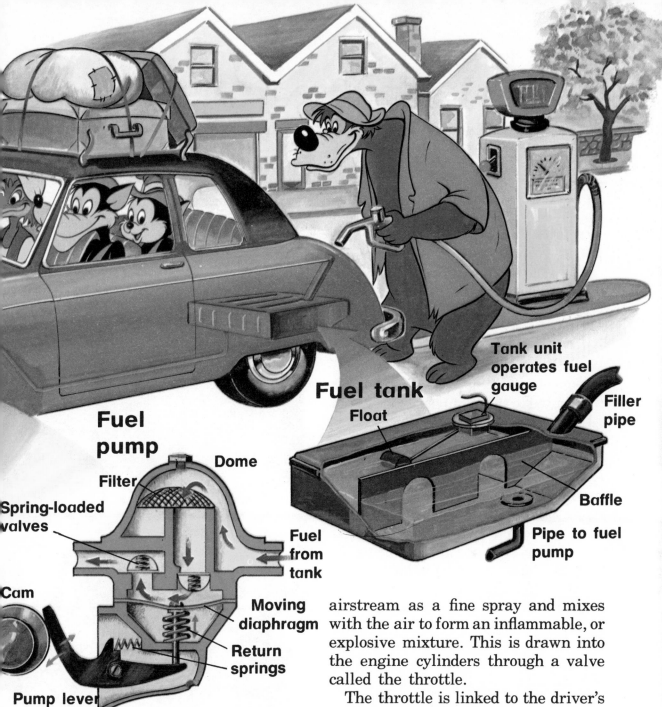

Fuel pump

Dome

Filter

Spring-loaded valves

Cam

Pump lever

Moving diaphragm

Return springs

Fuel tank

Tank unit operates fuel gauge

Float

Filler pipe

Baffle

Pipe to fuel pump

Fuel from tank

the float drops and the needle valve opens.

When the engine is running normally, air is sucked through the air filter into the carburetor. It speeds up as it passes through the narrow part of the carburetor tube, and sucks in gas from the outlet. The gas enters the airstream as a fine spray and mixes with the air to form an inflammable, or explosive mixture. This is drawn into the engine cylinders through a valve called the throttle.

The throttle is linked to the driver's accelerator pedal. When he steps on the accelerator, the throttle opens wider and lets more fuel mixture through to the engine cylinders. With more fuel to burn, the engine goes faster. Also, when the driver presses down the accelerator, an accelerator pump forces more gas into the carburetor tube through the accelerator jet.

Making Sparks Fly

The carburetor supplies a mixture of gas and air to the engine cylinders, where it is burned, or ignited. It is ignited by means of an electric spark, which is produced by the so-called ignition system. The most important part of the system is the battery, which provides the electricity to start with.

The battery supplies only low-voltage electricity—usually 12 volts —but to make a spark we need high-voltage electricity—of about 15,000 volts! This is produced by means of a coil and a contact-breaker. The high-voltage electricity is then passed on, or distributed to spark plugs in the engine cylinders, which produce the sparks. The device that distributes the electricity to the plugs is called the distributor. The distributor also houses the contact-breaker.

The car battery is completely different from the ordinary flashlight battery. It is a "wet" battery, which consists of plates of lead dipping into a solution of sulphuric acid. The lead combines chemically with the acid and produces electricity as it does so. The electricity is taken from the battery through contacts called electrodes. One is marked positive (+), the other negative (−).

The coil is an electrical device called a transformer. It contains two coils of wire wound on top of each other. One coil (primary winding) has few turns, the other (secondary winding) has many turns. The primary is connected to the battery and the contact-breaker. The secondary leads to the distributor head. When the engine is working, the

cam in the distributor continually opens and closes the contacts of the contact-breaker. This means that the electricity passing through the primary winding from the battery is switched continually on and off.

Every time this happens, a surge of

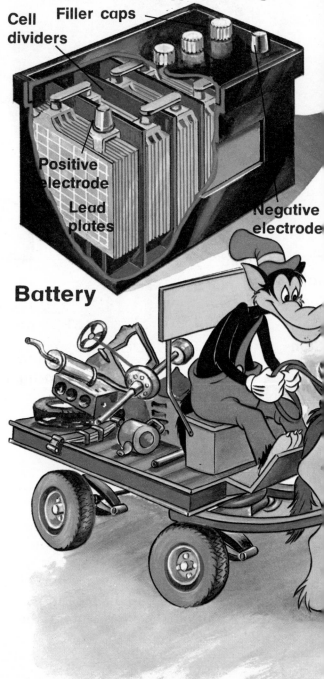

Cell dividers **Filler caps**

Positive electrode

Lead plates

Negative electrode

Battery

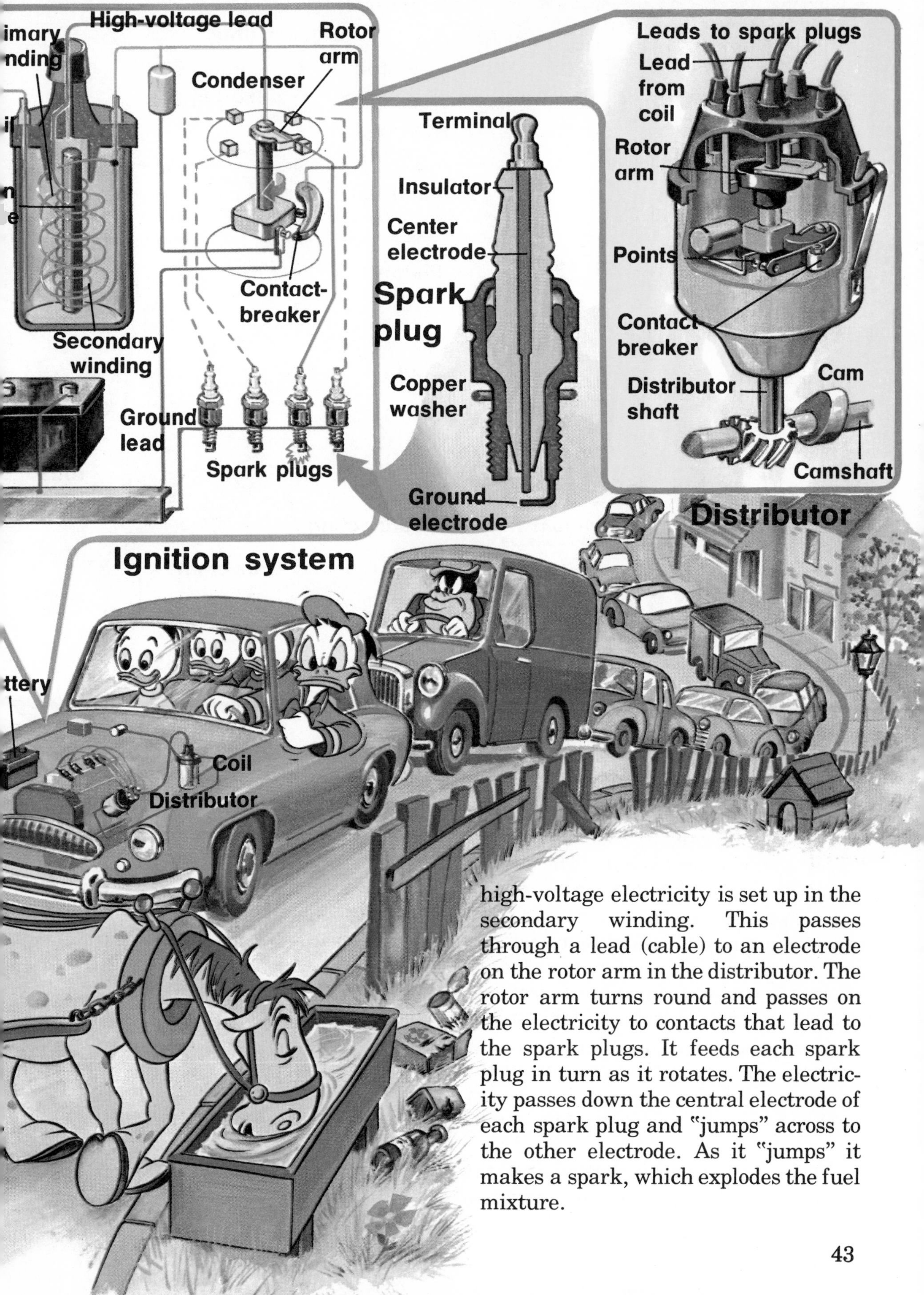

High-voltage lead

imary nding

Condenser

Rotor arm

il

e

Secondary winding

Ground lead

Spark plugs

Contact-breaker

Spark plug

Terminal

Insulator

Center electrode

Copper washer

Ground electrode

Leads to spark plugs

Lead from coil

Rotor arm

Points

Contact breaker

Distributor shaft

Cam

Camshaft

Distributor

Ignition system

ttery

Coil

Distributor

high-voltage electricity is set up in the secondary winding. This passes through a lead (cable) to an electrode on the rotor arm in the distributor. The rotor arm turns round and passes on the electricity to contacts that lead to the spark plugs. It feeds each spark plug in turn as it rotates. The electricity passes down the central electrode of each spark plug and "jumps" across to the other electrode. As it "jumps" it makes a spark, which explodes the fuel mixture.

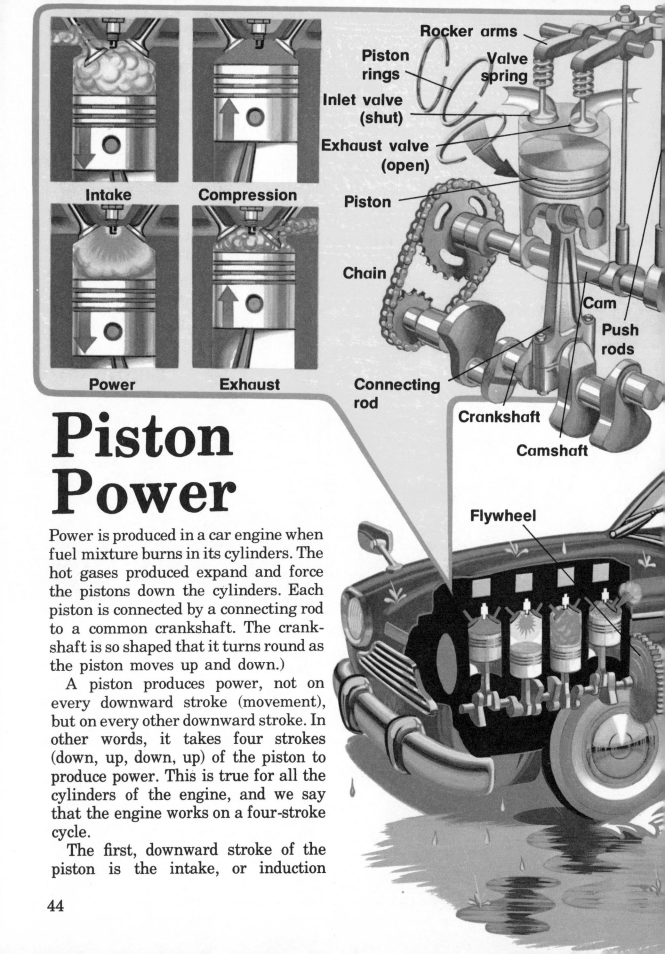

Intake

Compression

Power

Exhaust

Rocker arms

Piston rings

Valve spring

Inlet valve (shut)

Exhaust valve (open)

Piston

Chain

Cam

Push rods

Connecting rod

Crankshaft

Camshaft

Flywheel

Piston Power

Power is produced in a car engine when fuel mixture burns in its cylinders. The hot gases produced expand and force the pistons down the cylinders. Each piston is connected by a connecting rod to a common crankshaft. The crankshaft is so shaped that it turns round as the piston moves up and down.)

A piston produces power, not on every downward stroke (movement), but on every other downward stroke. In other words, it takes four strokes (down, up, down, up) of the piston to produce power. This is true for all the cylinders of the engine, and we say that the engine works on a four-stroke cycle.

The first, downward stroke of the piston is the intake, or induction stroke. Fuel mixture is sucked through an open valve (inlet) into the cylinder. The second stroke is the compression stroke. The piston moves up and squeezes, or compresses the fuel. Near the top of this stroke, the fuel is ignited. The gases produced drive the piston downward on its third, or power stroke. On the fourth and final stroke the piston moves upward again. The exhaust valve opens and the piston pushes the burnt gases from the cylinder. Next the exhaust valve closes, the piston moves down, and draws in fresh fuel mixture.

The valves which let the fuel mixture in and the exhaust gases out are opened and closed at the correct time by a rocking mechanism. It is driven from a camshaft, which in turn is driven by chain from the crankshaft. The camshaft has raised pieces, or cams on it. Resting on the cams are hollow tappets, into which long push rods fit. At the top, the rods touch one side of the rocker arm. When a cam rises, it pushes the tappet and push rod upward. This rocks the rocker arm, whose other side then pushes the valve open. When the cam falls, the push rod drops. The rocker arm rocks back, and the valve spring snaps the valve shut again.

The pistons deliver their power to the crankshaft in a series of "thumps." To make the engine run more smoothly, a heavy wheel is attached to the end of the crankshaft. It is called a flywheel. It helps store the energy provided by the pistons.

Keeping Cool

When gas burns inside the engine cylinders, a large amount of heat is produced. If it were not removed, the metal would expand, and the moving parts would lock together and not move. Keeping the engine cool is the job of the cooling system. Most car engines are cooled by water, but a few are cooled by air.

In a water-cooled engine the cylinder block and cylinder head contain passages through which cool water is pumped. The water carries away the heat produced when the fuel burns.

The hot water flows through a valve called a thermostat into the header tank at the top of the radiator. From

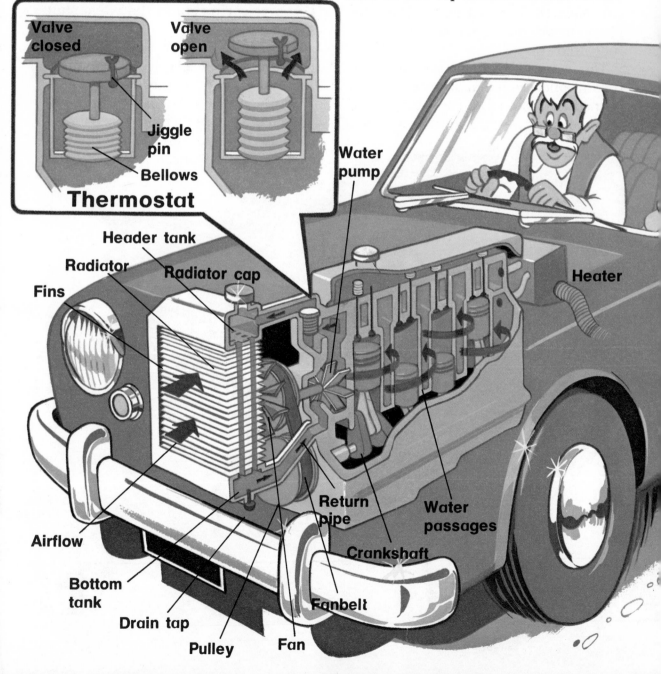

Valve closed

Valve open

Jiggle pin

Bellows

Thermostat

Header tank

Radiator

Radiator cap

Fins

Water pump

Heater

Return pipe

Water passages

Airflow

Crankshaft

Bottom tank

Drain tap

Fanbelt

Pulley

Fan

there it drops down through tubes to the bottom tank. The tubes are surrounded by metal fins. The network of tubes and fins is open so that air can pass through it and cool the water in the tubes. When the water reaches the bottom tank, it is cool enough to be pumped through the engine again.

opens and closes according to the temperature of the cooling water. When the engine is cold, the thermostat stays shut. This stops water going to the

radiator and allows the engine to warm up quickly. When the engine reaches its normal operating temperature, the thermostat opens. The water can then flow to the radiator to be cooled.

One kind of thermostat has its valve attached to a bellows containing liquid. When the liquid is cold, the bellows stay small and the valve is shut. When the liquid heats up, the bellows expands and opens the valve. Another kind of thermostat uses a metal rod containing wax. The valve is opened when the wax expands as it is heated.

In the winter a substance called antifreeze must be added to the water in the radiator. This stops the water freezing in frosty weather. If the water did freeze into ice, it could damage the engine. Ice takes up more space than water and can burst the pipes.

A fan helps draw the air through the radiator. It is driven by belt from a pulley on the end of the crankshaft. The water pump is mounted on the same shaft as the fan.

The valve called the thermostat

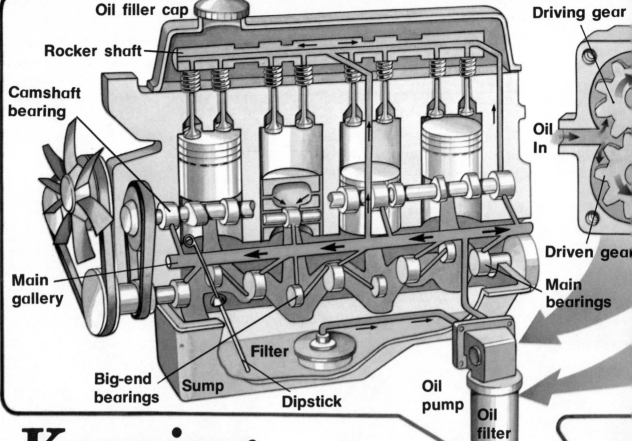

Oil filler cap
Rocker shaft
Camshaft bearing
Main gallery
Big-end bearings
Sump
Filter
Dipstick
Oil pump
Oil filter
Driving gear
Oil In
Driven gear
Main bearings

Keeping Well Oiled

A car engine contains as many as 150 moving metal parts. To keep them running smoothly, they must be kept well oiled. The oil stops the pieces of metal rubbing together. If they did rub together, they would become very hot and quickly wear out. The oil is provided by the car's lubrication system. ("Lubricating" is another word for "oiling.")

To main gallery

Supply from oil pump

Valve

Oil out

Oil pump

Casing

Paper filter

Oil filter

The oil is contained in a trough called a sump at the bottom of the engine block. From there it is pumped continually to all the moving parts. First it goes to a tube called the main gallery. From there it passes through narrow channels to the main bearings. These bearings support the crankshaft and allow it to turn. Channels inside the crankshaft then carry the oil to the bearings where the connecting rods are joined to the crankshaft. These bearings are known as "big-end" bearings.

From the main gallery other channels carry oil to the bearings supporting the camshaft and to the rocker shaft. The rocker shaft carries the rocker arms which open and close the valves (see page 44). The walls of the engine cylinders are oiled by oil flung off by the rotating bearings. All the oil drains back eventually to the sump.

The pump that pushes the oil through the engine is usually driven from a gearwheel on the camshaft. One common type is the gear pump, which consists of two gearwheels meshing together. The two gears revolve inside a casing and carry the oil around in the spaces between their teeth and the casing.

As the oil moves round the oil system, it gradually picks up bits of dirt and specks of metal. If they were not removed, the engine would quickly wear out. So two filters are included to remove them. One in the sump filters out the large pieces. The main filter is housed in a separate unit. It is usually made of specially treated paper. Usually the oil and filter need to be replaced about every 6,000 miles (10,000 km).

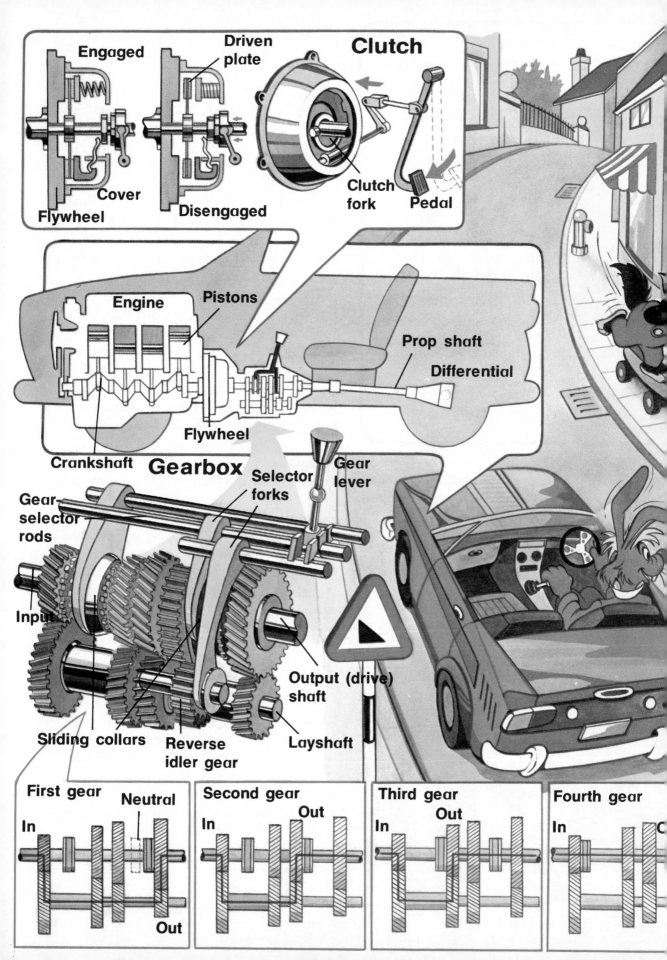

Clutch

Engaged

Driven plate

Cover

Flywheel

Disengaged

Clutch fork

Pedal

Engine

Pistons

Prop shaft

Differential

Flywheel

Crankshaft

Gearbox

Selector forks

Gear lever

Gear selector rods

Input

Sliding collars

Reverse idler gear

Layshaft

Output (drive) shaft

First gear

Neutral

In

Out

Second gear

Out

In

Third gear

Out

In

Fourth gear

In

Changing Gear

From the car engine, the power to turn the car's wheels is carried by the transmission system. Most cars have the engine at the front, and the driving wheels at the back. Then the transmission system is made up of clutch, gearbox, propeller shaft and final drive. This is the system illustrated here.

A driver needs his car to travel at many different speeds, from very slow when starting off to fast when he is traveling on the open road, but the engine only works well when it turns at certain speeds. To be able to drive the car at all speeds, different gears are used between the engine and the wheels. They are housed in the gearbox.

By changing gear, the driver moves different sized gearwheels together in the gearbox. This makes the shaft leaving the gearbox (the drive, or output shaft) turn at different speeds from the input shaft from the engine. He selects a low gear to start off. The output shaft then turns relatively slowly but powerfully. As the driver changes up into second, third and fourth gear, the output shaft turns faster and faster, making the car travel faster and faster.

There are two main sets of gearwheels in the gearbox. The gearwheels on the output shaft can be locked to it, one by one, by collars. These collars slide into position when the driver moves the gear lever. The other set of gearwheels is fixed to a layshaft. There is also a so-called idler gear in the box, which comes into play when the driver wants to reverse, or travel backward.

The driver cannot normally change gear while the engine is connected to the gearbox. If he tries to, the gearwheels clash together, making an alarming noise. Before he changes gear he has to disconnect, or cut off the engine from the gearbox. He does this by means of the clutch.

When the car is running normally, a plate on the end of the shaft going to the gearbox is pressed against the flywheel of the engine, and the gearbox shaft turns with the engine. When the driver presses the clutch pedal, the plate comes away from the flywheel, and the gearbox shaft is disconnected. The driver can then change gear without fear of the gearwheels clashing.

Final Drive

In most cars the gearbox is joined to the rear axle by a hollow tube called the propeller shaft, or prop shaft for short. Meshing gearwheels within the rear axle pass on the motion of the prop shaft to the rear wheels.

When a car is moving over a bumpy road, the gearbox and rear axle move up and down at different times. So the prop shaft joining them together must allow this to happen. It does so by having joints at each end which can bend in any direction. They are called universal joints. They consist of U-shaped yokes attached to a cross-shaped spider.

To allow for movement backward and forward, the shaft from the gearbox carries teeth, or splines. The coupling carrying the yoke can then slide along it when necessary.

The prop shaft joins the rear axle in a unit called the final drive. The final

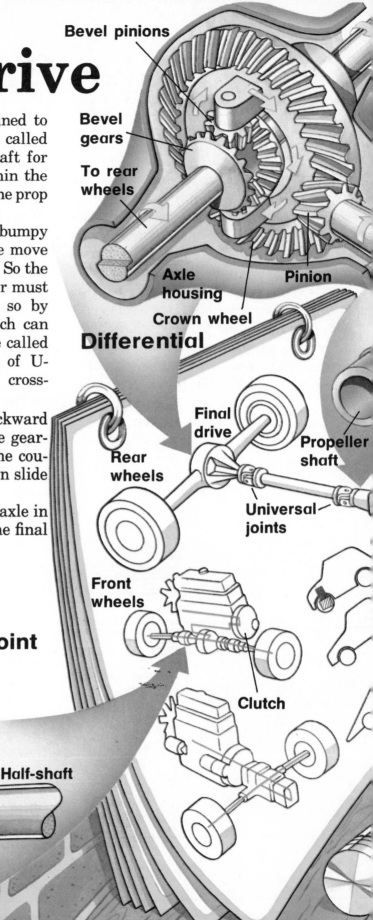

Bevel pinions

Bevel gears

To rear wheels

Axle housing

Pinion

Crown wheel

Differential

Final drive

Rear wheels

Propeller shaft

Universal joints

Front wheels

Clutch

Constant-velocity joint

Sockets

Ball-bearings

Half-shaft

Shaft to wheel

Cage

Splines

drive does several things. First, it changes the direction of the prop shaft's motion so that the wheels can be driven. Secondly, it acts as a gear to slow down the prop shaft, which is turning much too fast. Both these jobs are done by the crown wheel and pinion.

Shaft from gearbox

Propeller shaft

Splines

ke

Universal joint

Spider

The drive wheels are carried on two half-shafts on either side of the final drive. The crown wheel drives the half-shafts through an arrangement of bevel (angled) gears and pinions. Such an arrangement, called the differential, allows one rear wheel to turn more slowly than the other, if need be. This must happen, for example, when the car turns a corner. The inner wheel must move more slowly than the outer one, otherwise the car would skid.

Some cars have different kinds of transmission systems without a prop shaft. For example, they may have front wheel drive. They have the engine at the front which drives the front wheels. Often the engine is installed in a crosswise, or transverse position. It drives the wheels through a special kind of universal joint called a constant-velocity joint. Other cars have the engine at the rear which drives the rear wheels. Racing cars do, for example.

53

Disc brake

Bleed valve

Pads

Disc

Pistons

Pads   Disc

Studs

Hub

Piston housing

Pipeline

Brake-fluid reservoir

Foot pedal

Handbrake lever

Master cylinder

Disc brakes

Push rod   Pisto

54

Braking Hard

A modern car is able to travel at speeds up to 100 mph (160 km/h) or more, so it is very important that it has good brakes to slow it down quickly. To be on the safe side, all cars in fact have two braking systems.

The main one is worked by pressing down a foot pedal. It acts on all four wheels of the car. The second braking system is worked by pulling on a hand lever. It acts only on the rear wheels, and works by means of cables and levers.

The footbrake, on the other hand, works by means of hydraulic (liquid) pressure. When the pedal is pressed down, it pushes a piston connected to it along a cylinder ("master cylinder").

The piston forces liquid from the cylinder into pipes going to the brake units on the wheels. In these units the liquid pushes against pistons in smaller cylinders ("slave cylinders"). The pistons then force specially lined pads or shoes against the wheels, which slows them down. The pads and shoes have to be replaced from time to time when their linings wear out.

Most cars have two kinds of brakes. They have disc brakes on the front wheels and drum brakes on the rear wheels. In a disc brake unit, an iron disc is attached to the wheel and turns with it. Pistons force brake pads against both sides of the disc when the brakes are applied.

In a drum brake unit, an iron drum is attached to the wheel. When the brakes are applied, pistons force the ends of curved brake shoes outward. This makes them rub against the inside of the drum and slow it down. When the brakes are applied over and over again in a short time, they tend to "fade" or lose their power. This is because they get hot. Disc brakes are better than drum brakes because they do not heat up so much. Most of the disc is open to the air. Drum brakes are not as good because they are enclosed.

Drivers of very fast or heavy cars need to use a lot of effort to apply the brakes. This can become very tiring, especially on a long journey, so these cars are usually fitted with power brakes. Power brakes generally use the suction in the engine to help force the liquid through.

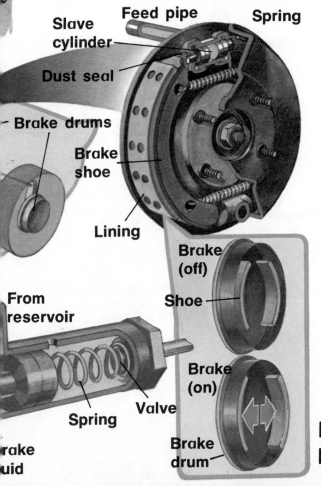

Slave cylinder
Feed pipe
Spring
Dust seal
Brake drums
Brake shoe
Lining
Brake (off)
Shoe
From reservoir
Brake (on)
Spring
Valve
Brake fluid
Brake drum

Drum brake

Steering

All cars are steered by turning the front wheels with a steering wheel. The diagram opposite shows a common type of steering system called rack and pinion. The steering wheel turns the steering column, at the end of which is a small toothed wheel, or pinion. The pinion meshes with a horizontal toothed rack, and the ends of the rack are connected to the front wheels.

When the steering column turns, the pinion also turns and moves the rack from side to side. Then the track rods turn the wheels. The wheels are attached to the car body by swivel joints so that they can turn easily.

The steering linkages are so arranged that the wheels always try to steer straight. Also, they make the inner wheel turn more sharply when the car is traveling around a bend. This prevents skidding and tire wear.

The air-filled tires of a car help cushion the passengers from bumps in the road, but their main job is to grip the road well in wet as well as in dry weather. To do this they have a deep tread cut in them. The tread provides grip and allows water to drain away.

The tire itself is made up mainly of rubber. It gets its strength from layers, or plies of tough fabric. These are wrapped around the tire in various ways. The tire shown has plies going

Tire

Breaker plies

Inner liner

Rim bead wire

Radial plies

Tread

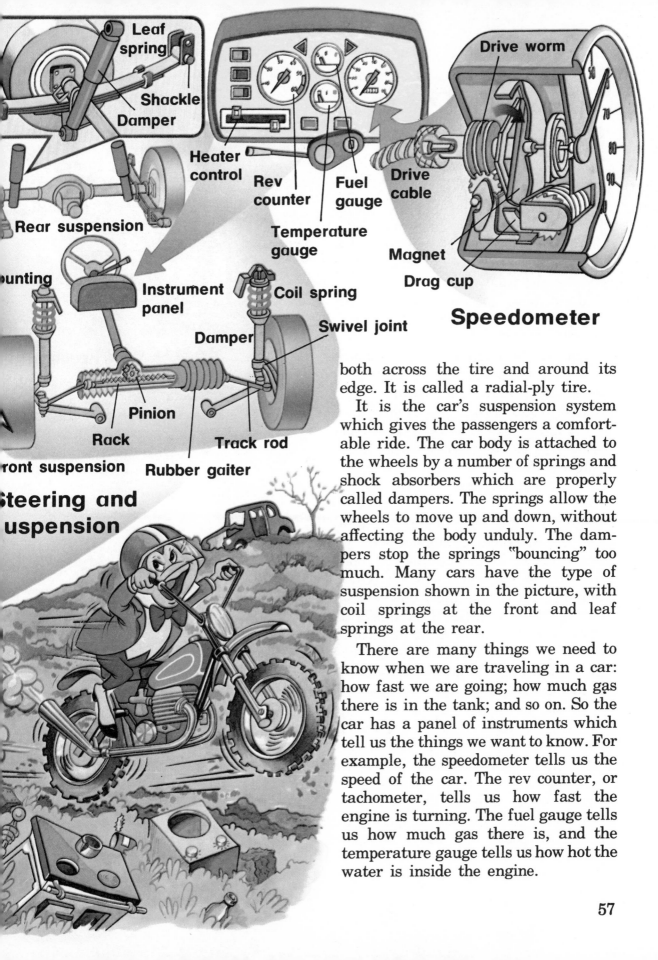

Leaf spring

Shackle

Damper

Rear suspension

Heater control

Rev counter

Fuel gauge

Temperature gauge

Drive cable

Drive worm

Magnet

Drag cup

Speedometer

...unting

Instrument panel

Coil spring

Swivel joint

Damper

Pinion

Rack

Track rod

...ront suspension

Rubber gaiter

...teering and ...uspension

both across the tire and around its edge. It is called a radial-ply tire.

It is the car's suspension system which gives the passengers a comfortable ride. The car body is attached to the wheels by a number of springs and shock absorbers which are properly called dampers. The springs allow the wheels to move up and down, without affecting the body unduly. The dampers stop the springs "bouncing" too much. Many cars have the type of suspension shown in the picture, with coil springs at the front and leaf springs at the rear.

There are many things we need to know when we are traveling in a car: how fast we are going; how much gas there is in the tank; and so on. So the car has a panel of instruments which tell us the things we want to know. For example, the speedometer tells us the speed of the car. The rev counter, or tachometer, tells us how fast the engine is turning. The fuel gauge tells us how much gas there is, and the temperature gauge tells us how hot the water is inside the engine.

On Two Wheels

Bicycles are a popular means of transportation. They move easily in traffic, take little space to park and do not use expensive fuel. The only energy they need is the rider's!

Motorbikes, or motorcycles, are really mechanized bicycles. They move much faster, of course, and can be very dangerous to operate. Helmets should be worn by motorcyclists and their passengers, and other safety rules should be followed. Motorbikes have gas engines which work in much the same way as car engines, with a few differences.

For example, most motorbike engines are cooled by air, not water. All around the engine cylinders there are metal fins, which become hot when the engine is working. The fins are cooled by air passing over them. To start a motorbike, the rider kicks down a lever called the kickstarter. This makes the engine start to turn. Most motorbikes are driven by chain from the gearbox. Some, however, do have a drive shaft, rather like a car's propeller shaft.

A rider controls a motorbike with his hands and feet. With one hand he controls the engine speed by means of a "twist-grip" throttle, and works the front brake lever. With the other hand he operates the lever that works the clutch. He uses his feet to operate the gearshift pedal and the rear brake pedal.

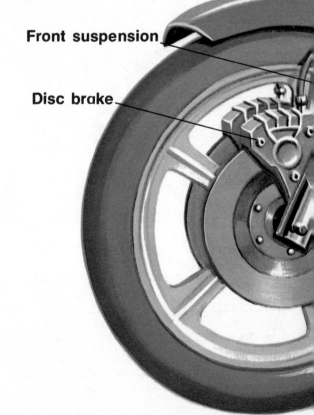

Headlight

Flashing indicators

Rocker shaft

Mudguard

Front suspension

Disc brake

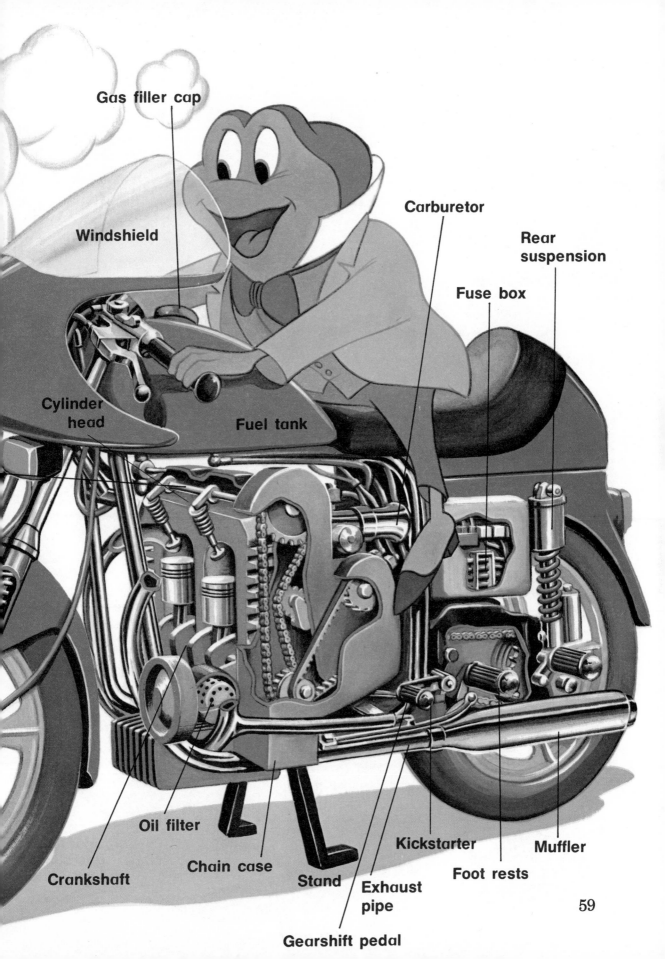

Gas filler cap

Windshield

Carburetor

Rear
suspension

Fuse box

Cylinder
head

Fuel tank

Oil filter

Crankshaft

Chain case

Stand

Exhaust
pipe

Kickstarter

Foot rests

Muffler

Gearshift pedal

59

GOOFY'S GARAGE

OFFICE

AIR

Gas tanker

Air line

Vent pipe

Tank valve

Suction pipe

Fill pipe

Underground gas-storage tank

OIL

Strainer

At the Garage

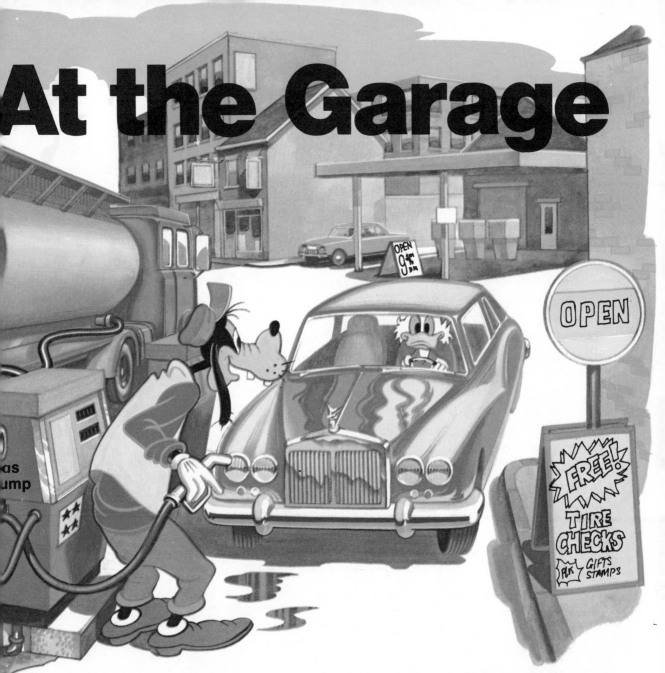

Although cars are much more reliable than they once were, they still have to be looked after, or serviced regularly. For example, the oil has to be changed when it gets dirty; the tires, when they wear down; and the exhaust pipe, when it rusts away. Some people can, and indeed love to, do the servicing themselves, but most of us have to take our cars to the garage or service station.

The garage is a fascinating place for those with a mechanical turn of mind. The mechanics use all kinds of hand and power tools to take a car apart and put it back together again. They use a block and tackle to lift out the engine, oxyacetylene torches to cut through and weld the metal body, and spray guns to apply paint. Most garage mechanics understand how cars operate and do good work.

The Gas Station

One thing we all need to go to the garage for is gasoline. It is kept in huge underground storage tanks, which are well sealed. Because gas is very inflammable, or burns easily, you must make sure no one lights a match or smokes a cigarette when your gas tank is being filled.

The attendant at the garage serves you with gas from a gasoline pump. The pump not only has to pump the gas into your tank from the underground tank, it also has to measure how much gas you are buying. A rotary pump, driven by an electric motor, pumps the gas first into the meter. In the meter a pair of pistons rock up and down and pump the gas steadily through the outlet pipe. The outlet pipe leads through a flexible hose to a metal nozzle with a "trigger" on/off switch, which the attendant puts into your tank.

The movement of the pistons turns a train of gears around, which turns the digits on two dials. One dial shows the volume (in gallons or liters) of gas being pumped into your tank. The other shows the cost of the gas. With the cost of gas being what it is, let us hope that your gas tank doesn't leak like the one in the picture.

Delivery nozzle

Air line

Air pressure gauge

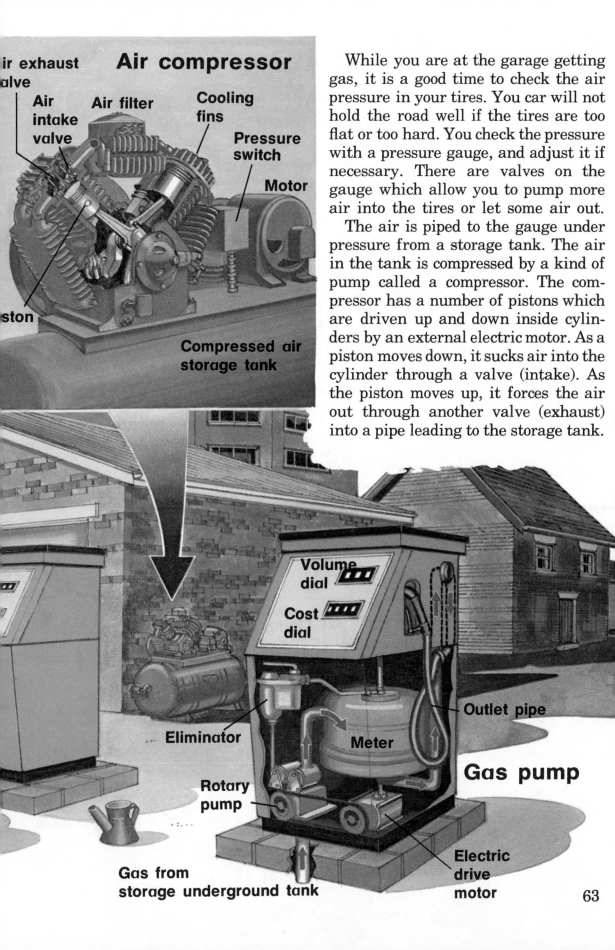

Air compressor

ir exhaust
alve

Air
intake
valve

Air filter

Cooling
fins

Pressure
switch

Motor

ston

Compressed air
storage tank

While you are at the garage getting gas, it is a good time to check the air pressure in your tires. You car will not hold the road well if the tires are too flat or too hard. You check the pressure with a pressure gauge, and adjust it if necessary. There are valves on the gauge which allow you to pump more air into the tires or let some air out.

The air is piped to the gauge under pressure from a storage tank. The air in the tank is compressed by a kind of pump called a compressor. The compressor has a number of pistons which are driven up and down inside cylinders by an external electric motor. As a piston moves down, it sucks air into the cylinder through a valve (intake). As the piston moves up, it forces the air out through another valve (exhaust) into a pipe leading to the storage tank.

Volume
dial

Cost
dial

Outlet pipe

Eliminator

Meter

Gas pump

Rotary
pump

Gas from
storage underground tank

Electric
drive
motor

63

Let us Spray

Compressed air is used in a garage for several other things besides pumping up tires. It is used for spraying paint, for example. When a car has been damaged in an accident, the metal panels of the body have to be hammered out and any dents filled. Usually a kind of plastic is used for filling, which gets very hard when it sets. This is then smoothed down and painted to match the color of the car.

Spraying is the best way of applying the paint. It is done by means of a spray gun, which is so called because it is held in the hand like a pistol and has a "trigger" switch. Compressed air enters the gun through a pipe in the handle, and eventually leaves through a fine nozzle in the front.

The gun works like a perfume spray. The tube leading to the nozzle is connected to a pipe carrying paint to the gun. As the air rushes past the pipe, it sucks paint from it. The paint mixes

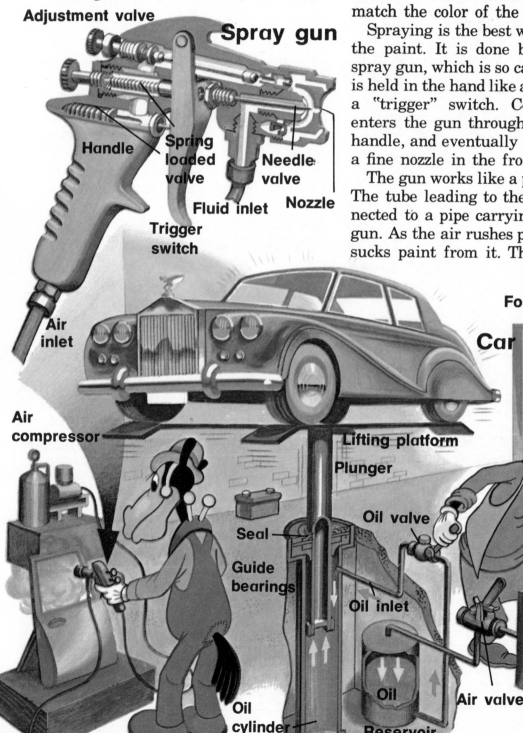

Adjustment valve

Spray gun

Handle

Spring loaded valve

Needle valve

Fluid inlet

Nozzle

Trigger switch

Air inlet

Air compressor

Lifting platform

Plunger

Seal

Guide bearings

Oil valve

Oil inlet

Oil

Reservoir

Air valve

Oil cylinder

Four post lift

Car lifts

with the air and forms a fine spray as it leaves the nozzle.

Quite often a mechanic needs to work underneath a car. He may have to do this the hard way by sliding underneath flat on his back through the mud and oil on the garage floor, but if the garage is better equipped, the mechanic raises the car rather than lowering himself. He does this by means of a car lift. This is a platform which can be raised and lowered. The car is driven on while the platform is at floor level. The platform is then raised to a suitable height to allow the mechanic to work in a comfortable standing position.

Two kinds of lift are shown here.

One has a single lifting arm and is worked by compressed air and oil pressure. It is really another hydraulic jacking device. For lifting, compressed air is allowed into the reservoir, which contains oil. The air pressure forces oil from the reservoir and into the lift cylinder beneath the car. Inside the cylinder the oil in turn pushes against a plunger carrying the lift platform and forces it upward. For lowering, the compressed air is let out of the reservoir. The oil can then flow from the lift cylinder back into the reservoir, allowing the plunger to drop.

In the other lift shown, the platform is lifted at all four corners. A motor lifts one corner directly. Then a cable and pulley system makes the other three corners lift at the same time.

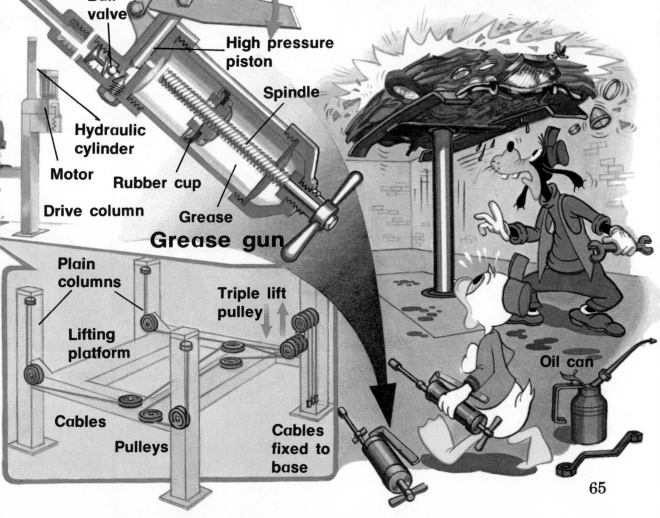

Ball valve

High pressure piston

Spindle

Hydraulic cylinder

Motor

Rubber cup

Drive column

Grease

Grease gun

Plain columns

Triple lift pulley

Lifting platform

Cables

Pulleys

Cables fixed to base

Oil can

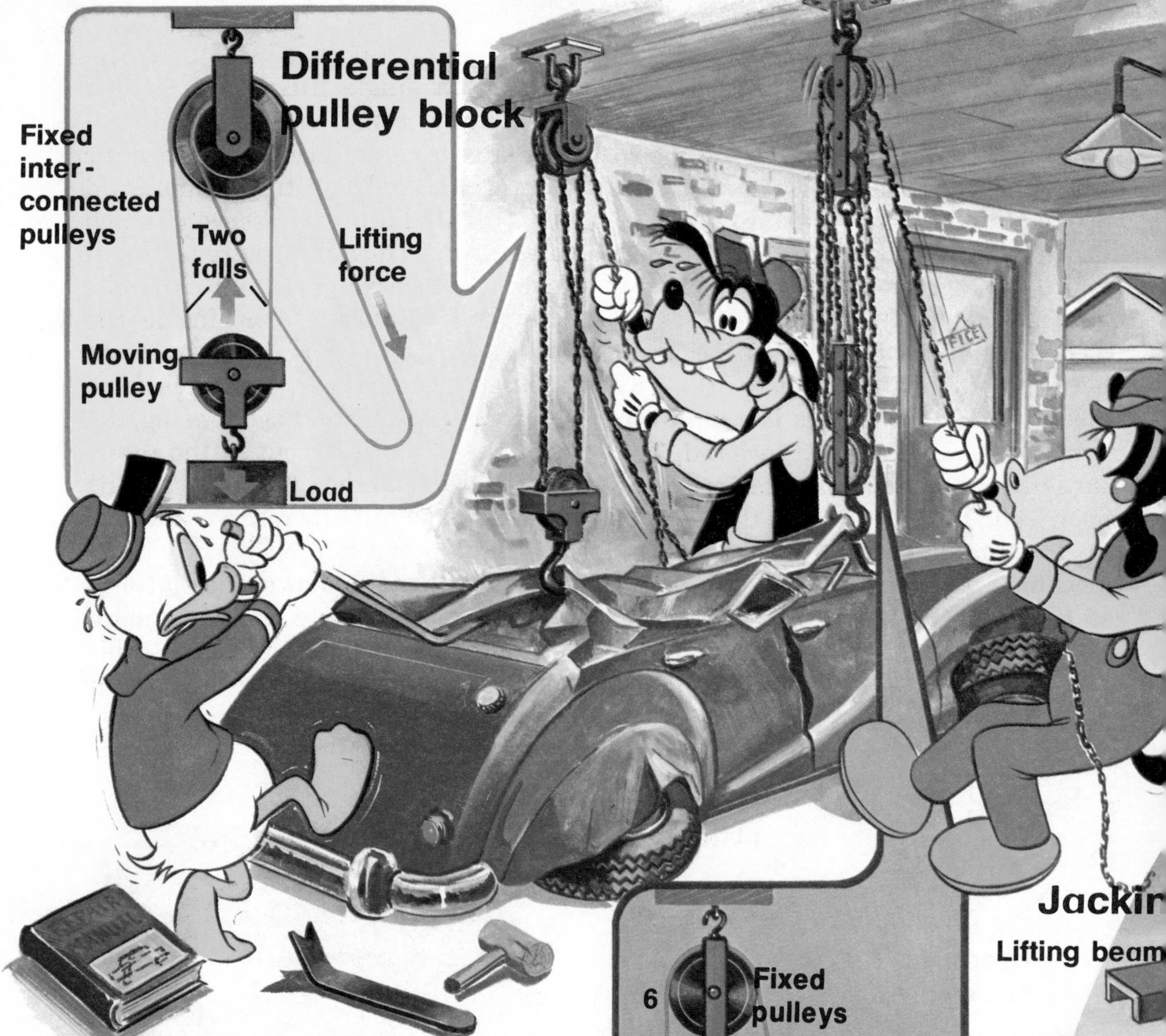

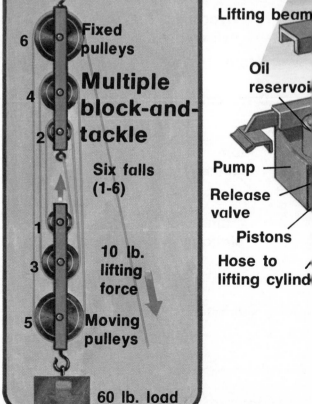

Differential pulley block

Fixed inter-connected pulleys

Two falls

Lifting force

Moving pulley

Load

Tackling the Job

Not all garages have hydraulic car lifts, of course. Perhaps this is just as well. Did you see what happened to the car on the previous page? The lift got out of control and squashed the car against the garage roof! This explains why on this page the garage mechanics

Multiple block-and-tackle

6

4

2

Fixed pulleys

Six falls (1-6)

1

3

10 lb. lifting force

5

Moving pulleys

60 lb. load

Jacking

Lifting beam

Oil reservoir

Pump

Release valve

Pistons

Hose to lifting cylinder

The block and tackle is one of the simplest of all machines. "Block" means the pulleys, and "tackle" means the ropes or chains passing around them. By using a block and tackle, you can lift a heavy load with less effort. It consists of two sets of pulleys – one fixed, the other moving. The fixed pulley block is hung from the roof or from an overhead beam. The load to be lifted is hung from the moving pulley block. The more pulleys there are in the system, the easier it is to lift the load.

The diagram on the opposite page shows a multiple block and tackle. The load is in effect supported by six ropes, or rather six "falls" of the same rope. So each "fall" carries one-sixth of the load. This means that you need only pull on the rope with one-sixth of the force you would need without a block and tackle.

Another type of block and tackle is shown at the top of the page, called a differential pulley block. The fixed block consists of two (or more) pulleys of different sizes connected together. The tackle passing over them forms an endless loop. Having the two different sized pulleys also makes lifting easier.

Also shown in the picture is a lifting jack, or jacking beam strong enough to support a car. Like the bigger car lift described on page 65, it works by hydraulic pressure. Oil is pumped from the reservoir to the lifting cylinder by working the pump handle back and forth. As the pressure in the cylinder increases, the ram is pushed out, forcing the lifting "scissor" arms upward.

The lifting arms are lowered by pressing the release valve. This allows oil to flow back into the reservoir from the cylinder, and the ram to return.

Pad

Inspection pit

eam

Extension arm

Ram

Lifting cylinder

Lifting arms

Pump handle

are shown trying to pull the car back into shape.

Garage mechanics don't often need to do this kind of thing, but they do often use the lifting gear shown here, the block and tackle. They use it for heavy lifting work, such as removing the engine from a car.

Breaking Down, Cleaning Up

In addition to their usual repair and maintenance service, many garages offer a breakdown service. If your car breaks down or is damaged in an accident, the garage will send a mechanic in a tow truck to help you.

If your car is steerable, the mechanic may simply attach a towline between a towbar on the truck and the front of your car. You get inside and steer the car while it is being towed. If the car cannot be steered, the mechanic will have to use the crane mounted on the back of the truck and lift up the front of the car for towing. The crane consists of a pair of struts, or booms, with pulleys at the top. Cables run up and over the pulleys from a winch to a crane hook, which is attached to the car. The winch turns the drums that wind up the cables. It drives the drums through a series of gears, while it is itself driven from the truck engine through a power take-off unit.

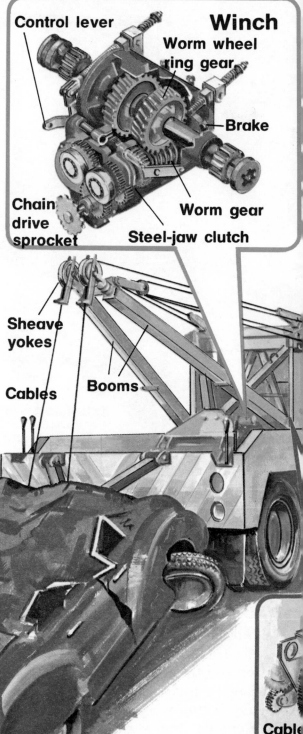

Control lever

Winch

Worm wheel ring gear

Brake

Chain drive sprocket

Worm gear

Steel-jaw clutch

Sheave yokes

Cables

Booms

Cable drum

If a car has been very badly damaged in a crash, it may not be worth repairing. Then it is regarded as being "totaled." The car we saw squashed against the garage roof on page 64 was totaled, and here you see it being towed away to a junkyard. There it will be looked over carefully, and any undamaged parts will be removed and later sold as "spares" for other cars of a similar make. The crumpled body shell remaining will then be crushed as small as possible and taken with other scrap to the steelworks. There it will eventually be resmelted and made into fresh steel.

Pulleys

Tow truck

CAR WASH

Moving gantry

Roof brush

Side brushes

Motor

Hydraulic cylinder

Water system

AJK 579C

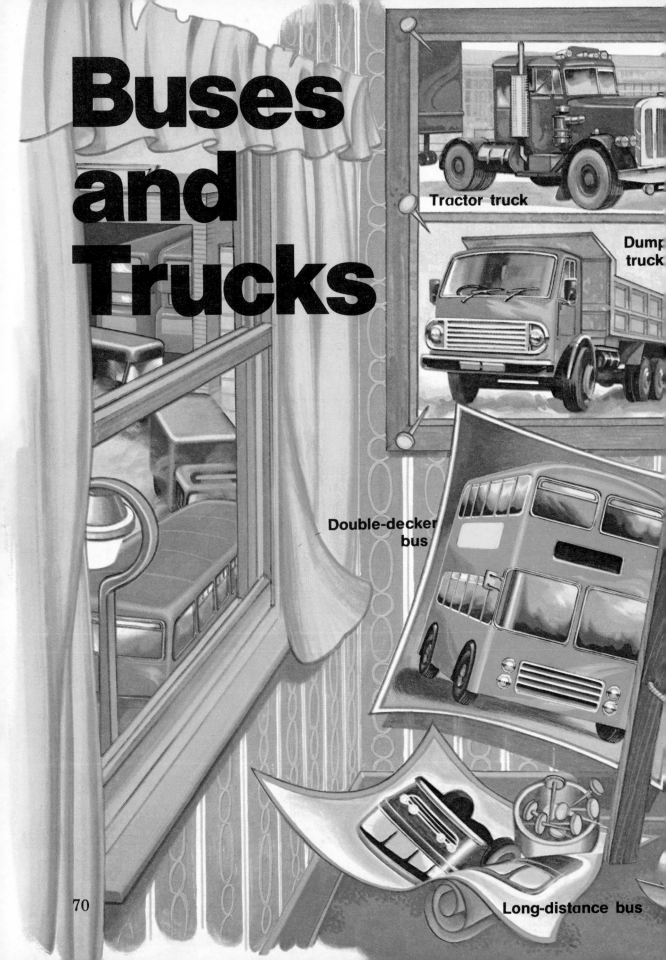

Buses and Trucks

Tractor truck

Dump truck

Double-decker bus

Long-distance bus

70

Antique bus

Trailer truck

One of the best ways to travel around the city is by bus. It is usually quite cheap and very convenient. You don't have the problem of parking, as you would if you traveled by car. Also, people who travel by bus help reduce traffic congestion. A double-decker bus can carry up to 60 passengers, while taking up the space of only about three cars!

The bus is one of the so-called commercial vehicles, which are used for transporting the public or carrying goods of one kind or another. Other commercial vehicles include many types of trucks, garbage trucks, street cleaners and milk trucks. Mechanically these vehicles work in much the same way as a car, but with one important difference. They usually have a diesel engine, which burns oil, rather than a gas engine.

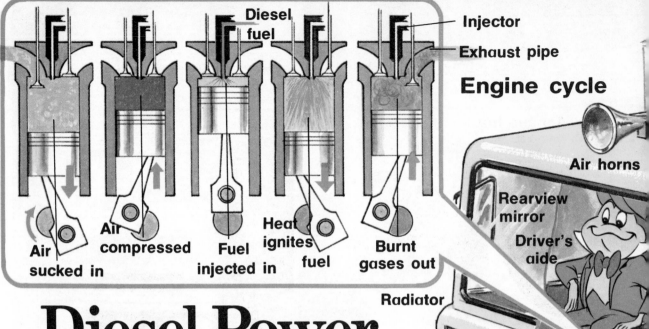

Diesel
fuel

Injector

Exhaust pipe

Engine cycle

Air
sucked in

Air
compressed

Fuel
injected in

Heat
ignites
fuel

Burnt
gases out

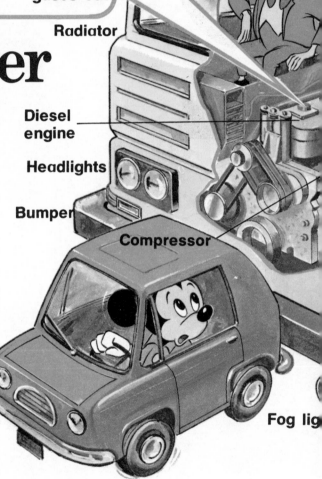

Air horns

Rearview
mirror

Driver's
aide

Radiator

Diesel
engine

Headlights

Bumper

Compressor

Fog lig

Diesel Power

The trucks that carry goods on our roads can be huge. Pulling trailers, they can be as long as a house and weigh almost as much.

The engine most heavy trucks have is a diesel engine, built with pistons and cylinders in much the same way as a car engine, but it works differently. For one thing, it burns a kind of light oil called diesel oil, not gas. Also, this fuel is injected directly into the engine cylinders and does not go through a carburetor. Also the fuel is exploded by heat and not an electric spark.

The engine works on the same kind of cycle, or sequence of piston movements as the gas engine – the four-stroke cycle (see page 44). This is what happens in each cylinder in turn: On the first down stroke of the piston, air is drawn into the cylinder. The piston next moves up and squeezes, or compresses, the air so much that it becomes very, very hot. Fuel is then injected into the hot air, and immediately explodes. The explosion pushes the pis-

ton down, producing power. When the piston moves up again, it pushes the burnt gases from the cylinder. Then the cycle is repeated.

As in a car, a transmission system

72

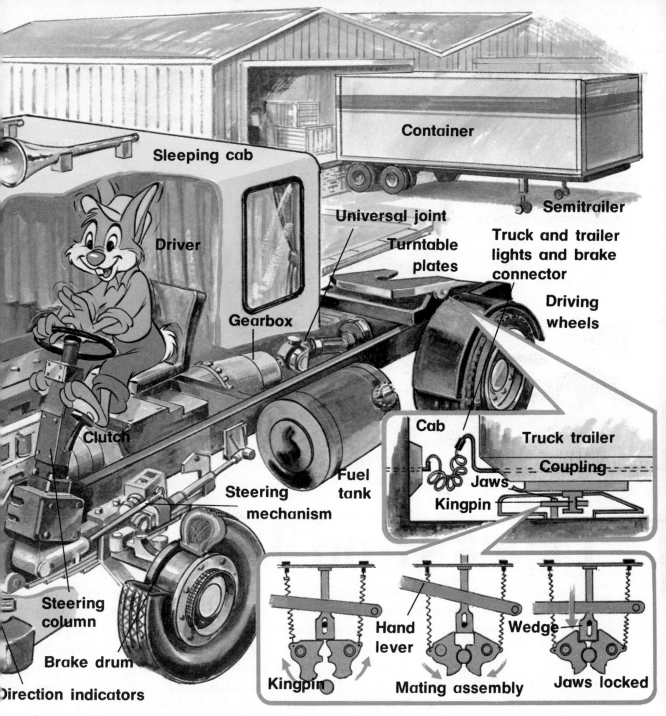

Container

Sleeping cab

Semitrailer

Driver

Universal joint

Turntable plates

Truck and trailer lights and brake connector

Driving wheels

Gearbox

Cab

Truck trailer

Coupling

Jaws

Kingpin

Clutch

Fuel tank

Steering mechanism

Steering column

Hand lever

Wedge

Brake drum

Kingpin

Mating assembly

Jaws locked

Direction indicators

(page 50) carries power from the engine to the driving wheels. Most truck transmissions are similar to that of a car, and have a clutch, gearbox, propeller shaft and final drive. The main difference is that the gearbox generally has many more gears. Some heavy trucks can have as many as 30 forward gears and 3 reverse gears!

Most trucks have power brakes to help them stop quickly. They use power from the engine rather than the driver's muscles. Some are hydraulic (liquid pressure) brakes like those on cars. Others are air brakes, which are much more powerful. When the driver presses the brake pedal, compressed air forces the brakes on.

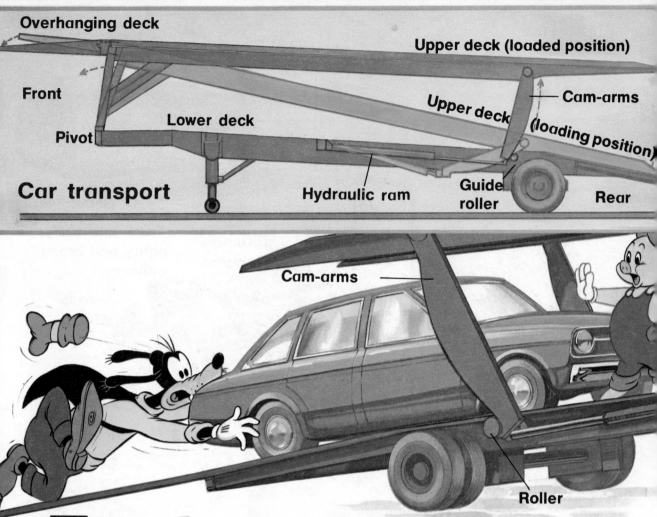

Car transport

Overhanging deck

Upper deck (loaded position)

Front

Upper deck (loading position)

Cam-arms

Lower deck

Pivot

Hydraulic ram

Guide roller

Rear

Cam-arms

Roller

Trucks and Trailers

A truck is built in a different way from a car. Most cars have a one-piece body, to which the engine and wheels are joined. A truck, however, is usually built with a basic frame, or chassis, and a separate body. The chassis unit consists of strong steel girders which carry the engine, wheels, transmission and driver's cab. Then different kinds of bodies can be built on the chassis, perhaps by a different company.

A common kind of body is the drop-side body. It has one side which can be lowered for loading and unloading. Another is the tipper body, which unloads by tipping up. Some trucks

have enclosed bodies, like furniture vans and cattle trucks. Others have bodies designed for a special purpose. One is the container loader, which has a flat body and hydraulic arms to lift heavy containers on and off it. Other special trucks include garbage trucks (page 78) and street-cleaning machines and sewer cleaners (page 80).

All the trucks mentioned so far have fixed bodies, and the longer they are, the more awkward they are to turn, or maneuver. To make maneuvering easier, some trucks are designed with a swiveling body. They are called articulated trucks. They consist of a tractor

Supporting legs

Hydraulic ram

Truck tractor

and a semitrailer. The tractor is like the front part of an ordinary truck, with engine, cab and short chassis on four or six wheels.

The semitrailer has one or more pairs of wheels at the rear, but at the front it overlaps the tractor. It is connected to the tractor by a coupling which allows for swiveling movement. The coupling is shown on page 73. When the semitrailer is uncoupled, it rests at the front on supporting legs, which hinge down.

There are several special articulated semitrailers. One is shown above: it is a car transport. It can carry several medium-sized cars on two decks. The two decks are joined together by pivoting struts at the front and cam-arms at the rear. The upper deck is lowered at the rear for loading, and then lifted by hydraulic rams. The rams push the cam-arms over the guide rollers, and this forces the upper deck upward. The hydraulic pressure to power the rams comes from a pump unit in the tractor.

Lift, Mix, Tip and Dump

The upper deck of the car transport just described is raised and lowered by hydraulic jacks. Many other trucks use hydraulic jacks. These jacks are supplied with liquid under pressure from a hydraulic pump on the truck.

The most common use for hydraulic equipment in trucks is for tipping. The

Crane

Crane hook

Protective frame

Mast

Chain pulley

Cement mixer

Fork carriage

Hydraulic lifting jack

Tilt jack

Transmission

Drive wheel

Diesel engine

Radiator

Fuel tank

Hydraulic pump

76

that the load can be emptied easily, without the need for a tailgate.

Two other kinds of special heavy trucks are the mixer truck and crane carrier. The mixer truck has a body like a cement mixer, and it does mix cement. Cement, sand, gravel and water are poured into the mixing vessel just before the truck starts its journey to the construction site. While the truck is traveling, the body rotates. By the time the truck has arrived on site, the cement is mixed, ready to be poured. The crane carrier is a truck with a crane mounted on it. The crane

Tower crane

Dump truck

Hydraulic jack

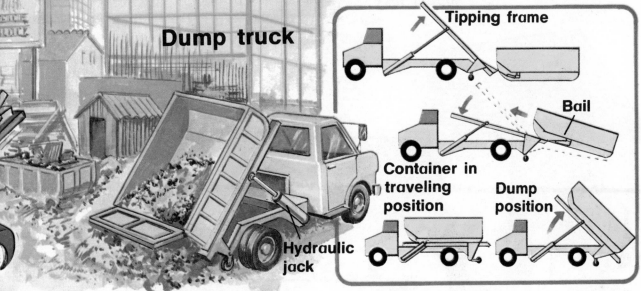

Tipping frame

Bail

Container in traveling position

Dump position

body of the tipper truck is mounted so that it can tip up to empty its load. It is hinged near the rear and is forced up at the front by powerful hydraulic jacks. The rear body section, or tailgate, opens to allow the load to escape. The container tipper shown above carries its load in separate containers, which are emptied by a tipper frame.

In road building and other heavy construction work, a much more rugged tipping truck is used, called a dump truck. It is shallow at the rear so

may be operated from the driver's cab or from a separate control cabin. Hydraulic pumps power the hoisting mechanism and the telescopic crane arm, or boom. In operation the truck rests on "feet" for firm support.

The forklift truck shown is used for lower and lighter lifting duties. It carries loads on a two-pronged fork at the front. The fork carriage is moved up and down a mast by a chain and pulley mechanism, which is powered by a hydraulic jack.

orklift truck

Trash and Garbage

Practically everything we eat, drink or use these days comes to us packaged in paper, cardboard, plastic bags, bottles or cans. Afterwards, all this packaging material is thrown away in garbage cans or trash bags along with bones

Hopper — **Packer plate rises**

Packer plate — **Hopper lifts**

Trash storage — **Packer plate removes rubbish from hopper**

Tailgate — **Tailgate rises, ejecti ram expels trash**

Tailgate

Tailgate lifting ram

Packer plate

Hopper

Ejection ram

and scraps of food left over from meal-times and ashes from the fire. Each of us on average produces about 5 lb (2 kg) of trash of one kind or another every week.

In most populated areas, this trash is collected by a trash collector, or garbage truck, and taken to a site out of town, where it is eventually disposed of. The garbage truck is a special vehicle with an enclosed body (to keep in the smells!) and rams for compressing the garbage as it is tipped in, and later for emptying it.

What happens to the trash is shown in the series of pictures on the opposite page. The garbage men empty the garbage cans into the hopper. A hydraulic ram then raises the packer plate (1), and the hopper is lifted (2). Next the packer plate moves down, compresses the trash, and scoops it into the body (3). The hopper is then lowered ready to receive more rubbish.

When the garbage truck is ready to be emptied, the tailgate is raised. Then the ejection ram pushes the trash out. In some cities the trash is not simply buried, but put to good use. It is first sorted, and things like cans, bits of metal and glass are removed from it. The rest is burned in a furnace. The heat produced can then be used to heat buildings or even produce electricity. The metal is sent for scrap and eventually will be remelted and used again. This re-use, or recycling of materials is becoming more and more necessary, because the world's mines will one day run out.

Gas, too, will one day run out. Then many cars will run on electricity, like the milk trucks of England do today. The electricity is provided by batteries, and turns an electric motor which drives the wheels.

Milk Truck

Electric motor

Drive axle

Batteries

Wash Up and Brush Up

The garbage truck (page 78) is just one of the special vehicles used by local government authorities to keep our towns clean and neat. Another is the street cleaner shown here. This is a kind of mobile vacuum cleaner, which "vacuums" the roads.

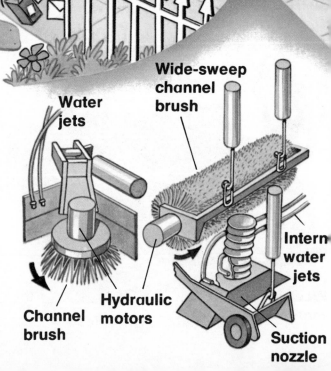

Wandering hose

Fan system

Auxiliary engine

Inlet pipes

Water jets

Wide-sweep channel brush

Internal water jets

Channel brush

Hydraulic motors

Suction nozzle

Most of the dirt, leaves, paper and other trash on our roads ends up in the gutters. If it were allowed to stay there, it would not only look messy, but also block up the drains and possibly cause flooding.

The street cleaner moves along the road slowly, a few inches from the curb. It has a small round brush that sweeps right up to the curb, and a long brush that sweeps further out. The

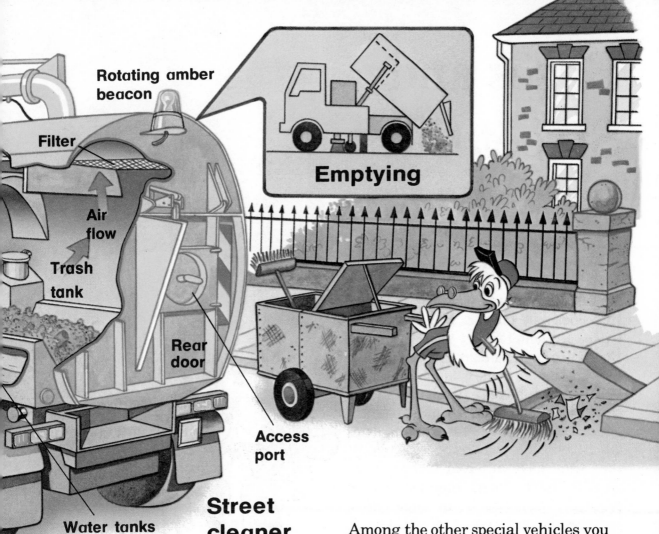

Rotating amber
beacon

Filter

Air
flow

Trash
tank

Rear
door

Access
port

Emptying

Water tanks

Street
cleaner

swept-up dirt is sucked up through a
hose into the trash tank. The suction is
produced by a powerful fan, worked
from a separate, or auxiliary engine.

To help the cleaning process and
settle the dust, water is sprinkled on
the road as it is being swept. It is
sprayed from water jets supplied from
tanks at the sides of the vehicle.

A hydraulic pump provides liquid
under pressure to spin the motors that
turn the brushes. It also provides
power for the hydraulic jacks attached
to the sides of the trash tank. The jacks
are extended to tip up the tank for
emptying.

Among the other special vehicles you
can see in the city is the sewer cleaner.
This is used to pump water from
blocked drains, or sewers. It has a long
suction hose attached to an arm that
swings out from the body. An engine-
driven pump sucks water up the hose
and delivers it to a large storage tank.
This forms most of the body of the
vehicle.

In frosty weather the sanding truck
will be out. It carries a load of fine
gravel or sand, mixed with salt. It
scatters this gravel on the road by
means of a disc device. The gravel falls
on to the disc, which is rotating, and is
flung outward over the road. The
gravel gives tires better grip on the icy
roads, while the salt helps melt the ice.

Buses and Street Cars

In the country the best way to travel is by car, but in the city it is usually better to travel by bus. One great advantage of traveling by bus is that you never have any parking problems. School buses are not as comfortable as long-distance buses (see page 84), but this does not matter, because people travel on them for only short journeys. Buses are built to hold as many people as possible. Some "double-decker" buses, which have seats on two levels, can carry more than 70 passengers.

Transit and travel buses are built in much the same way as trucks, except that they have different bodies. They usually have diesel engines, which drive the rear wheels. In some cities, however, a different kind of bus is used, called a street car or trackless trolley. This runs on rubber-tired wheels, like an ordinary bus, but it is driven by electric motor.

The street car picks up its electricity from a pair of overhead conductor wires. It makes contact with these wires through two poles on its roof. The poles are sprung and pivoted so that the bus can move from side to side beneath them. The bus can only move a little way, however, otherwise the poles will come off the wires.

Trolleys work by electricity picked

Street Car

Bus

Street car motorman

Lights

Rails

Overhead wire

Overhead wire

Trolley pole

Hook

Current collector

BUS STOP

Doors

Wheels

Passengers

up from overhead wires, but the trolley has steel wheels and runs on a pair of rails, like a train. Because it runs on rails, it does not need as much power as a trolley bus. Friction between steel wheels and rails is very low. The drawback with trolleys, however, is that they cannot move from their fixed path to weave in and out of the traffic.

Usually trolleys have only a single trolley pole, making contact with a single overhead wire. The second wire of the electrical circuit is provided either by the rails themselves, or a cable beneath a slot in a center rail.

A special kind of street car is found in San Fransisco, called a cable car. The passenger cars are hauled along by a moving cable traveling in a slot beneath the track. The car driver uses a clutch to grip the cable when he wants to move.

83

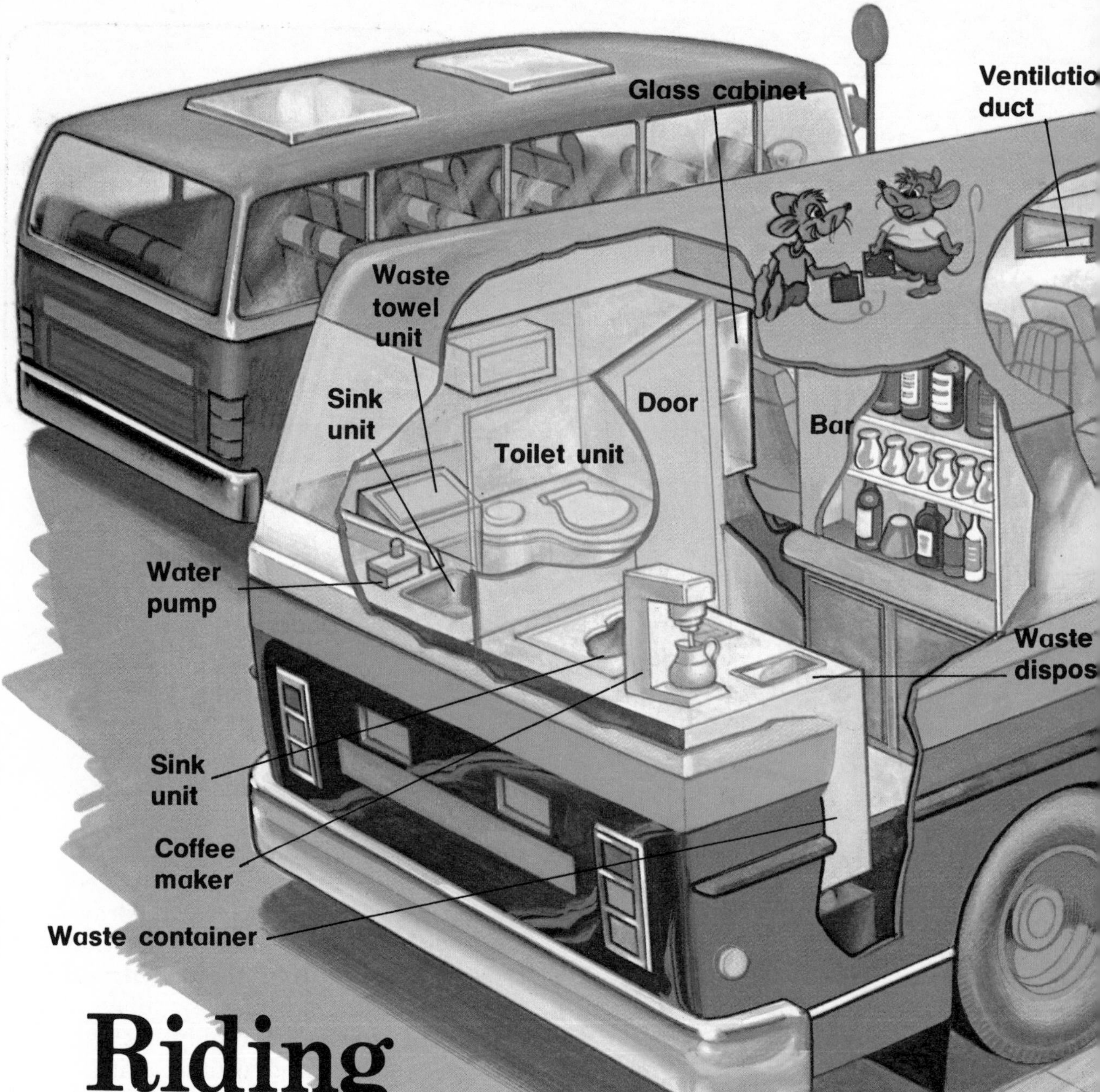

Glass cabinet

Ventilation duct

Waste towel unit

Sink unit

Door

Bar

Toilet unit

Water pump

Waste disposal

Sink unit

Coffee maker

Waste container

Riding in Comfort

The buses that carry you around town are not the most comfortable of vehicles. If you intend to travel a long way, then you will need to be more comfortable. Modern buses are being designed with this in mind.

Seats in these long-distance coaches are well-padded, and have headrests on them. They are reclining seats, which means they can tilt backward to give you greater comfort or help you to snooze! In some coaches some seats are spaced so as to leave room for tables. The whole floor level of these coaches is very much higher than that of ordinary

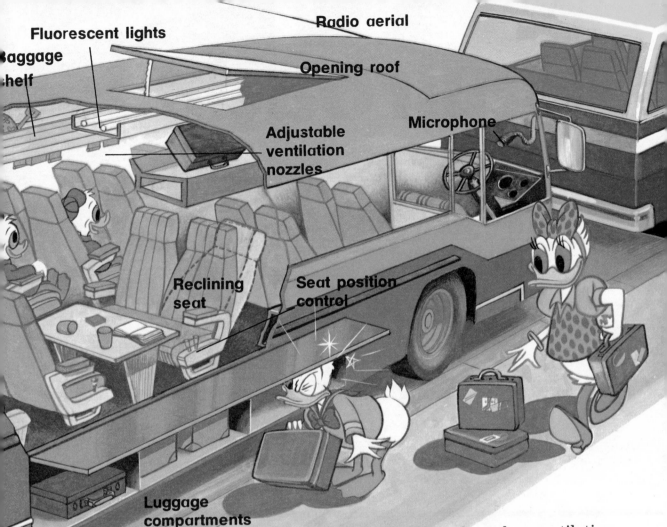

Fluorescent lights

Baggage shelf

Radio aerial

Opening roof

Adjustable ventilation nozzles

Microphone

Reclining seat

Seat position control

Luggage compartments

buses and the windows are bigger. This allows you a better view of the passing scenery. The windows are often tinted green to cut down the glare when the sun shines.

In the sunshine too the bus could become unbearably hot on a long journey. So it is air-conditioned, which means that the air inside the coach is continually freshened. The hot, smoky, stale air is passed through an air conditioner, which cools it and removes any smoke and smells. The now fresh air is then returned to the passenger compartment through ventilation ducts. There are often little ventilation nozzles over each seat, which you adjust to blow air where you want it.

Also for your comfort, the bus has at the rear a washroom with a toilet. This is very necessary when the bus travels nonstop for several hours. If you feel thirsty you can get yourself a cup of coffee, or something else to drink at the bar.

On scenic routes and guided tours the driver explains points of interest through a loudspeaker system. He speaks into a microphone mounted on a flexible arm in front of him. He may have a two-way radio on board as well, and report from time to time to his base or speak to his fellow drivers.

Railroads

The railroads have been with us now for over 150 years. They are not as important as they once were because many people now prefer to travel by car and send goods by truck, but when the trains carry a full load, railroads are a very efficient form of transport. Thanks to new high-speed electric and diesel trains, the railroads now provide very fast service.

In cities the railroad stations are at their busiest in the morning and evening rush hours, when millions of commuters crowd into them.

In some cities railroads run underground as well as on the surface. They are often called subways. It is usually quicker to travel across town by subway than by car or bus, because it avoids the traffic jams in the streets.

At the Station

The main railroad station in a large city is busy for most of the day and often during the night as well. Busiest are the great terminals in cities like New York, London and Paris. From these terminals ("ends" of the lines) trains arrive from and depart to other cities throughout the country. The largest station of all is Grand Central station, which is built on two levels and on which there are a total of 67 railroad tracks. It covers an area of nearly 50 acres.

These large stations are almost like shopping centers. They may have different shops, banks, restaurants, bars, book stores and newstands. In contrast, a small country station may consist of no more than a ticket office and a vending machine.

Handling passengers is one of the two main jobs the station has to do. The other is handling goods and luggage. Ticket sellers are on hand at the ticket office to issue tickets. At the information desk they will give you advice on your traveling problems. There are porters to carry your bags for you.

Large boards list the arrival and departure times of the trains, and a station announcer tells you over the loudspeaker when the trains will depart, from which platform they will leave, and where they will stop on their journey.

At the station, when the train has arrived, baggage is unloaded and put on carriers to be taken to the platforms where it will be picked up. The cars are cleaned and food and drink are taken on board. The baggage, mail and cargo are loaded into the baggage and mail cars.

If you want to get to a station in a hurry, then a taxi is often the best way to do so. Taxi drivers know all the short cuts and the best way to avoid heavy traffic. Their meter charges you for the distance you travel and also for time when the taxi is waiting ie traffic. The meter mechanism is driven by a cable from the taxi's wheels and by a clock.

Unit arm
held up

Camshaft

Unit
arm

Mileage
counter

...umping
...m

Flag

Fare
drum

**Taxi
meter**

Flag gears

Meter
drive shaft

ARRIVALS

SWEETS and TOB...

NOTICE

Electric
baggage
mover

Getting up Steam

Until about 20 years ago most trains were hauled by steam locomotives, but only a few "steamers" are still working regularly, in parts of South America, Africa and Asia. Elsewhere steamers can be seen on privately owned railroad lines, run by steam enthusiasts.

The mainline steam locomotive is a huge machine, built of iron and steel and weighing 100 tons or more. It can thunder along at speeds of 100 mph (160 km/h) or more, spitting out fire, steam and smoke like a dragon.

In a steam locomotive coal is burned in a furnace, producing flames, smoke and hot gases. They rise into the firebox and are then drawn through tubes running through the boiler. The tubes are surrounded by water, which is heated so much that it boils into steam. The steam collects in the steam dome at the top of the boiler and is

Points motor
Detector
From signal box
Points control box
Points
Signal control relays
Signal
Track-circuiting equipment
Shunting engine
PLATFORM 1
Coal bunk
Tende

delivered by a pipe into the cylinders.

In each cylinder the steam pushes against a piston which is joined by a connecting rod to a crank on one of the driving wheels. It is joined in such a way that when the piston moves back and forth, the wheel is turned around. Coupling rods link this wheel to the other driving wheels.

After the steam has pushed the piston one way along the cylinder, the slide valve moves across and admits steam to the other side of the piston and the piston is forced back again. When the steam leaves the cylinder, it escapes through the blast pipe and then up through the chimney. As it does so, it helps pull the hot smoke and gases through the boiler tubes.

In a mainline steam locomotive the coal for the furnace and the water for the boiler are carried in a tender behind. In the small shunting (switching) engine, however, coal is carried in a small bunker behind the driver's cab, and water is carried in tanks on each side of the boiler. This kind of locomotive is often called a tank locomotive.

Trains move from one track to another with the help of points (switches). A set of points is a pair of curved rails linking the two tracks. One end is movable, and is moved across to direct the train's wheels one way or the other.

Chimney

Blast pipe

Steam dome

Firebox

Steam delivery pipe

Boiler tubes

Lagging

6231

Buffers

Lights

Brake shoes

Slide valve

Connecting rod

Cylinder

Piston

Driving wheels

Sand pipe

Reclining seats

Baggage car

Cooling unit

Diesel engi

Batteries

Diesel Trains

Today two kinds of locomotives dominate the railroad scene – diesel and electric, but diesels can travel on any track. Electric locomotives can travel only on electrified track.

The most important kind of diesel is the diesel-electric. It is so called because it uses a diesel engine to drive an electricity generator, and the electricity then powers electric motors which turn the driving wheels.

The diesel engine which drives the generator works in the same way as a truck diesel engine, explained on pages 72 and 73, but it is much more powerful. Whereas a truck diesel engine has a power output of about 100-200 horsepower, a locomotive diesel engine may have a power output of over 3,000 horsepower! To produce such power, each engine is much bigger and also has a fan or a blower, to force extra air into the engine. The fan is driven by a turbine in the engine exhaust pipe.

This method is called turbo-charging.

The train illustrated is an English High-Speed Train, which at present holds the world diesel rail speed record of 143 mph (230 km/h).

There are two other kinds of diesel locomotives. One is called the diesel mechanical. It is really a bus on rails because it uses a clutch and gearbox to transmit power to the driving wheels.

The third kind of diesel locomotive is the diesel hydraulic. Power is transmitted from the diesel engine to the driving wheels by means of a hydraulic (liquid) coupling. The coupling is a device called a torque converter, which

High-speed train
Inter-City 125

Electricity generator

Driver's cab

Controls

Horns and lights

Electric traction motors

is a kind of turbine, filled with oil. Similar couplings are used in the automatic transmission systems of cars.

Electric Trains

Diesel trains can travel fast, but not as fast as electric trains. Some electric trains are already running that can reach speeds of over 150 mph (240 km/h). The drawback about electric trains is that they need a special track to run on – a track that has been electrified.

A track may be electrified in two ways. It may be done by laying an extra, or third rail alongside the existing track. The electric locomotive then picks up its electricity from this rail by means of a sliding contact "shoe."

A track may also be electrified by means of overhead wires. This is the most common way. The locomotive picks up the electricity from the wires by a sprung arm contact on top of the cab. This is called a pantograph.

The electricity in the overhead wires is at the very high voltage of up to

Level-crossing gates

Fiberglas nose co

Pantograp

Brake air reservoir

Gangway connection

25,000 volts – over 100 times that of the ordinary electricity fed to our homes. This is much too high for the electric motors that must drive the locomotive, so first the voltage has to be reduced. This is done by a transformer.

Also the electricity picked up by the locomotive is alternating current (AC). This means that the current surges continually back and forth through the wires. This is fine for heating and lighting at home, but not for powering the traction motors. It has to be changed into one-way (direct) current electricity, like that which comes from a battery. A device called a rectifier does this.

In a normal electric train the suitably changed electricity is fed to traction motors. These drive the wheels, which are mounted in a frame, or bogie, directly by means of simple gears. In one modern train, however, a different arrangement is used. This train is the Advanced Passenger Train (APT) of British Rail, in England.

The APT, unusually, has motors that drive its wheels by means of a shaft and gearbox. It has other unusual features, too. One is that it tilts when going round corners, allowing it to take them very fast. Another is that it has exceptionally powerful water brakes, which work like a water turbine in reverse.

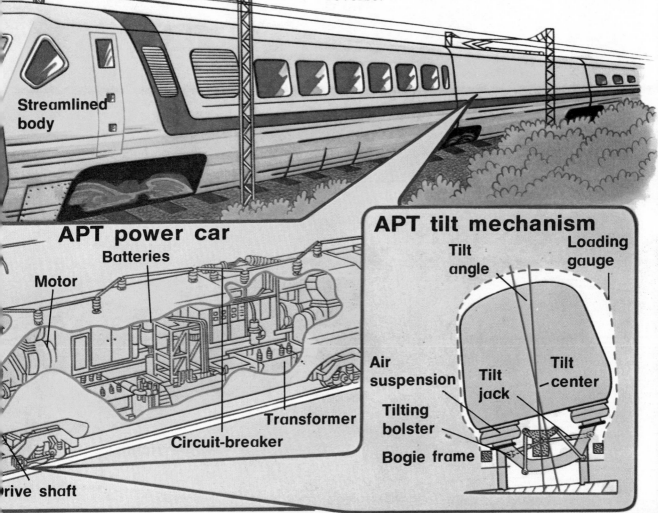

Overhead power lines Power pylons

Streamlined body

APT power car

Motor
Batteries
Transformer
Circuit-breaker
Drive shaft

APT tilt mechanism

Tilt angle
Loading gauge
Air suspension
Tilt jack
Tilt center
Tilting bolster
Bogie frame

Container Terminal

Engage

Disengage

Legs

Motor generator

Grapple and tilt unit

Freight container

Rotates

96

Many goods are carried these days by road, rail and sea in containers. These are large wooden crates of standard size. It is a very convenient way of carrying goods of many different shapes and sizes. Special lifting equipment has been designed to move containers between trucks, railroad cars and container ships. It is a kind of giant crane, which can handle containers weighing up to 30 tons.

The main structure consists of two pairs of legs connected by cross girders. Both legs and girders are long welded-steel "boxes." The two pairs of legs span a distance of some 50 feet (15 meters), or about three railroad tracks and one road. They are themselves mounted on a railroad track by means of a two-wheeled unit, so that they can move from car to car along a train.

Running on wheels along the top of the cross girders is a traveling carriage, or crab. This carries the hoisting mechanism for lifting the containers. The containers are suspended from a so-called grapple and tilt unit, which is located at the end of a rigid hoist mast.

The driver's cage is also attached to the crab unit, and from its twin consoles he can control all lifting and moving operations. Since the loading and unloading of containers carries on 24 hours a day and in all weather, the cab is comfortable. It has an upholstered chair, a built-in heater, and demisting equipment and windshield wipers.

The leg units, the traveling crab and the hoisting mechanism are powered by electric motors. The electricity is produced, or generated, by a large motor generator. Sometimes this is driven by a diesel engine.

In operation, the driver moves the crab until the hoisting gear is directly over the container to be moved. Then the container is attached, hoisted and carried by the traveling crab over to where it is to be transferred. In skillful hands the equipment can handle up to 360 containers in a day.

Control consoles

Slew
Tilt
Travel
Hoist
Supply
Emergency stop
Grapple-lifting centers
Hydraulics

Coupling

Buffer

Buffers Spring

Safety First

When you are driving a car and see something in your path, you can either put on your brakes and stop quickly or swerve out of the way. When you are driving a train, however, things are not so easy. Because the train is very heavy, it takes quite a long time to stop after you apply the brakes, and you cannot swerve out of the way of something in your path because you run on a fixed track.

The railroads must therefore insure that two trains are never approaching one another, or are close together, on the same track. They do this by signaling. Alongside the railroad tracks are signals which tell the engineer whether to "stop" or "go." They are controlled by a signalman in a signal box. The signalman knows of all the trains approaching or leaving his section of the track, and he can set the signals accordingly. He also controls the crossover points so that he can switch trains from one track to another.

In the past railroads used semaphore signals, which had movable arms on tall posts. The position of the arm told the driver of a train whether to "stop" or "go." These signals were set by the signalman pulling on large levers. The signalman used to receive and pass on information about the trains by means of electric telegraphs.

Today, however, most signals are colored lights, much like road traffic lights. They show green for "go" and red for "stop." Some consist of lights in rows set at various angles like

semaphore arms in two positions. One or the other row is lit up to signal "stop" or "go."

In a modern signal box, like the one shown here, the signalman controls a much longer length of track than he used to. All the signals and all the points are set by pressing buttons or flicking switches. The signalman receives and passes on information about the trains by telephone. To give

Map of railroad tracks

Telegraphs

Operating levers

nal Caution Line
clear

nger

Illuminated
indicator panel

ntrol panel

him a clearer picture of what is happening on the tracks, there is an
illuminated indicator panel in the box.
It carries a map of the railroad tracks
outside, which lights up wherever
there is a train.

99

Making Tracks

The track on which the trains run has to be very carefully laid. The two rails that form the track must be as level as possible and exactly the right distance apart. The distance they are apart is called the track gauge. The standard gauge is 4 ft. 8½ ins (143.5 cm). Some railroads in other countries run on a broader gauge; others on a narrower gauge of 3 ft 3 ins. (1 meter).

To build the track, large numbers of rails have to be joined together. They may be joined with fishplates, as the picture shows. A small gap is left

Joining the rails

Bolts

Fishplate

Rails

Fishplate

Nuts

Warning flag

Maintenance gang

Instrument for checking track gauge

between them so that they can expand when they become hot. Rails may also be joined together by welding. In welding, the ends of the rails to be joined are heated red-hot, and then molten metal is run into the gap between them. When the metal cools, it hardens and forms a strong joint. Sometimes several miles of track are continuously welded together. This allows a much smoother and quieter ride.

The rails rest on iron baseplates, which are fixed to wooden or concrete sleepers. The sleepers spread out the weight of the train over a large area. The baseplate and rails may be fixed to the sleeper by spikes, nuts and bolts, or by clips.

Baseplate

Rail

Clips

Sleeper

Baseplate

Baseplate

Sleeper

Ballast

Busy Lines

On modern railroads the trains are getting faster and faster—on some lines they run at speeds up to 150 mph (250 km/h). When trains travel that fast, the track takes a great pounding, for trains are very heavy things, so railway engineers must check the track regularly to see that it is always in perfect condition. This means not only checking the rails themselves, but also the track bed beneath the sleepers.

The rails tend to flex, or bend a little when a train goes over them, and they bend back again when the train has gone. When this is repeated time and time again, it can cause weakness, or fatigue in the metal. After a while this may cause a thin crack to appear in the metal, which could develop into a serious crack and eventually make the line break. If this happened while a train was passing, the train would be derailed, and a major disaster would occur.

To prevent this kind of thing, the rails are often checked by ultrasonic scanners. These devices send high-pitched sound waves through the metal. If there is a flaw in it, this will show up on instruments. Other instruments in a special track-recording car check that the rails are level and properly lined up. If they are not, the railroad track gang is called in to put things right.

The railroad track rests on sleepers which lie in a bed of stone chippings, or ballast. There are several reasons for having ballast. It distributes the weight of the train over a larger area of the track bed. It holds the sleepers in position, and it serves to drain water from the track. When the track has to be leveled, the rails and sleepers have to be lifted, and then ballast has to be added or removed from underneath. The track is then replaced and the ballast is pounded or tamped down to make it settle.

Lifting, leveling and tamping down are done mainly by machines. Machines are also used to keep the ballast clean. If the ballast were allowed to become clogged up with oil and dirt, it would not drain properly. The track might then become waterlogged, which could cause accidents. Ballast cleaners like the ones shown here are fitted with scoops, conveyors and lifting and lining devices. They lift up the track, remove dirty ballast, clean it and replace it, while moving slowly along the track.

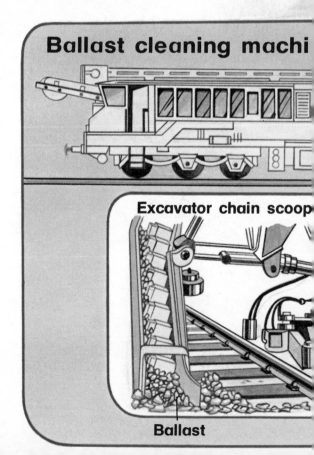

Ballast cleaning machi

Excavator chain scoop

Ballast

Lifting and lining device

Scoop

Stripper frame

Air-cushion monorail

Jet engine

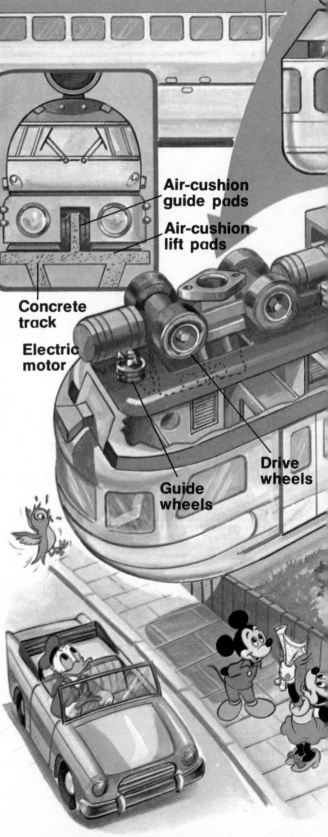

Air-cushion guide pads

Air-cushion lift pads

Concrete track

Electric motor

Drive wheels

Guide wheels

One Rail Only

Some new railroads are being built, not with tracks of two rails, but with tracks of a single rail. They are called monorails (mono means one). Some monorail trains run along the top of the track. Others run underneath it – they are called suspension monorails.

One kind of suspension monorail train is shown here. On top of the passenger cars are sets of wheeled units called "bogies." These run inside a hollow box-like beam. The four main wheels of the bogie are driven round by an electric motor. Sets of smaller guide wheels at the sides keep the bogie in the center of the track. Another kind of suspension monorail hangs beneath the track on an arm.

Some monorails that run along the top of the track are driven and guided by wheeled bogies like the ones described above. Others are driven and guided in a much more advanced way. The air-cushion monorail train literally flies a few inches above the track. Air is blown beneath the train and

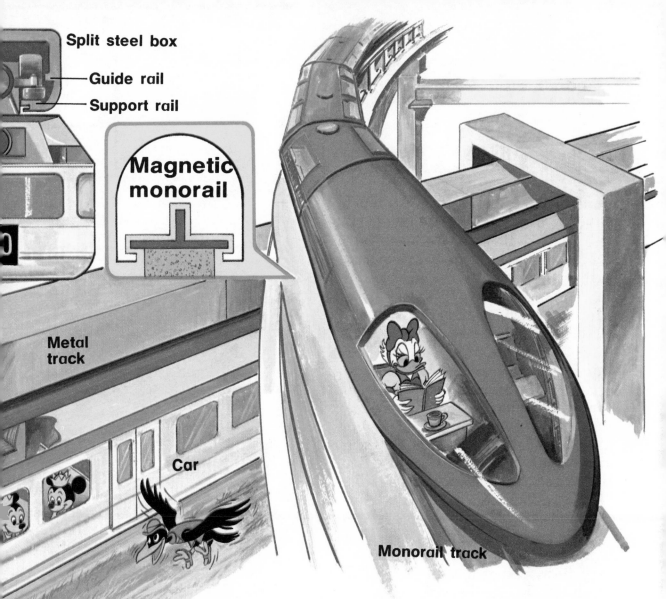

Split steel box

Guide rail

Support rail

Magnetic monorail

Metal track

Car

Monorail track

Suspension monorail

raises it above the track. Once it is out of contact with the track, it can be propelled very fast. The one shown is driven by a jet engine. It can reach speeds of 235 mph (380 km/h) – much faster than any ordinary train.

Another interesting kind of monorail is lifted above the track and propelled by magnetism. It is called a maglev monorail. "Maglev" is short for "magnetic levitation" (magnetic lifting). Many experts believe that the maglev monorail will be the train of tomorrow.

A maglev train carries on board a powerful magnet. When it is moving above a metal track, it makes the track itself become magnetic. The magnetism of the train magnet and the track act in opposite directions and raise the train above the track. The train is propelled by a different kind of electric motor called a linear motor.

Going Under the Ground

Generally, railroad systems throughout the world are being reduced in size to help make them more economical to run, but one type of railroad system is expanding. This is the underground railroad, or subway. It is easy to see why this is happening, for the city streets above ground are becoming more and more clogged with traffic as time goes by.

Although underground rail systems are new to some cities, others have had them for a century or more. Oldest of all is London's Underground, which dates back to 1863. It is also still the biggest, with more than 250 miles (400 km) of track.

In the early days, underground railroads were worked by specially designed steam locomotives. They were very filthy things to ride on, because much of the smoke and steam got trapped in the tunnels, but in the 1890s the underground 'went electric'. They

Air cylinder

Rack

Door

Piston

Sprung loaded arm

Sliding doors

Paris Metro system

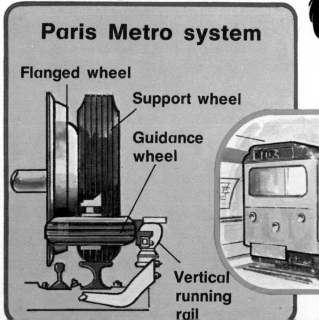

Flanged wheel

Support wheel

Guidance wheel

Vertical running rail

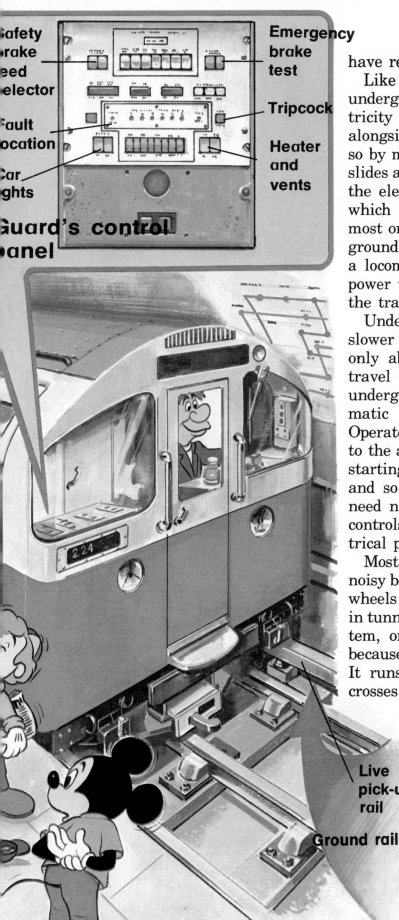

Safety brake
Speed selector

Emergency brake test

Tripcock

Fault location

Heater and vents

Car lights

Guard's control panel

Live pick-up rail

Ground rail

have remained electric ever since.

Like some surface electric trains, underground trains pick up their electricity from a third "live" rail laid alongside the ordinary track. They do so by means of a contact "shoe" which slides along the live rail. From the shoe the electricity goes to electric motors which turn the train wheels. Unlike most ordinary trains, however, underground trains are not hauled simply by a locomotive in the front. They have power units spaced at intervals along the train.

Underground trains travel much slower than ordinary trains, averaging only about 25 mph (40 km/h). They travel quite close together along the underground tracks and rely on automatic signaling for safe working. Operators control the train according to the automatic signals, stopping and starting it, opening the sliding doors, and so on. Some of the latest trains need no operators at all! A computer controls everything by means of electrical pulses in the rails.

Most underground systems are very noisy because of the clatter of the steel wheels on the steel rails in the closed-in tunnels. The Paris underground system, or Métro, is quieter than most because it runs on rubber-tired wheels. It runs on its steel wheels when it crosses over points on to another track.

Pick-up shoes

Stairs on the Move

Some underground railroads are constructed from the surface. Great trenches are dug and then concreted over to form tunnels. This method is known as "cut and cover." It was used, for example, to build Paris's underground railroad – the Métro. It was possible there because many of the streets are straight and wide. The resulting tunnels are only a few feet below ground level, and can be easily reached by a few flights of stairs.

The cut and cover method cannot be used in most cities, however, where the streets are fairly narrow and winding and heavily built-up. Tunneling must be carried out deep down in firm ground. In London, for example, the

Data roll

Ejection roller

Display board

Print drum

Ticket

Inker

Coin box

Feed disc

Guides

Ticket roll

Ticket machine

Escalator

Guide pulley

Handrail

Tension wheel

Endless chain

Inner rails

Step

Return pulley

Rachet wheel

Bottom wheels

108

tunnels are dug in the firm clay that exists beneath the city. They are bored by tunneling machines with circular cutting heads. The tunnels have to follow the layer of firm clay and sometimes go as far as 200 ft (60 meters) below the surface.

When underground stations have to be that far down, the passengers would be exhausted if they had to climb stairs to reach street level, so deep stations usually have elevators to transport passengers to and from the surface.

As long as the station is not too far down, a better solution is to have one or more escalators. An escalator is a moving staircase. It works continuously and can carry ten times as many passengers as an elevator.

The steps of the escalator are connected on either side to endless chains. These are driven by toothed drive wheels powered by an electric motor. The moving handrail is also driven

Comb plate

Electric motor

Worm gear
Drive wheel
Returning steps

Outer
rails

Top
wheel

Top wheels
Outer rail

Steps
Inner
rail

Bottom wheels

noice
lection
ys

from the same drive shaft. The step carries two pairs of wheels which run in rails. The rails are positioned so that the steps form stairs traveling upward, then flatten out at the top and stay flat until they return to the bottom.

Other machines at the stations help speed the flow of passengers. They include ticket machines and automatic turnstiles. The machine shown issues tickets of different value. The ticket is printed when the correct money is inserted. The printed ticket is placed in a slot in the turnstile. If it is the correct ticket, the gate or "stile" turns and you can enter and go to your train.

109

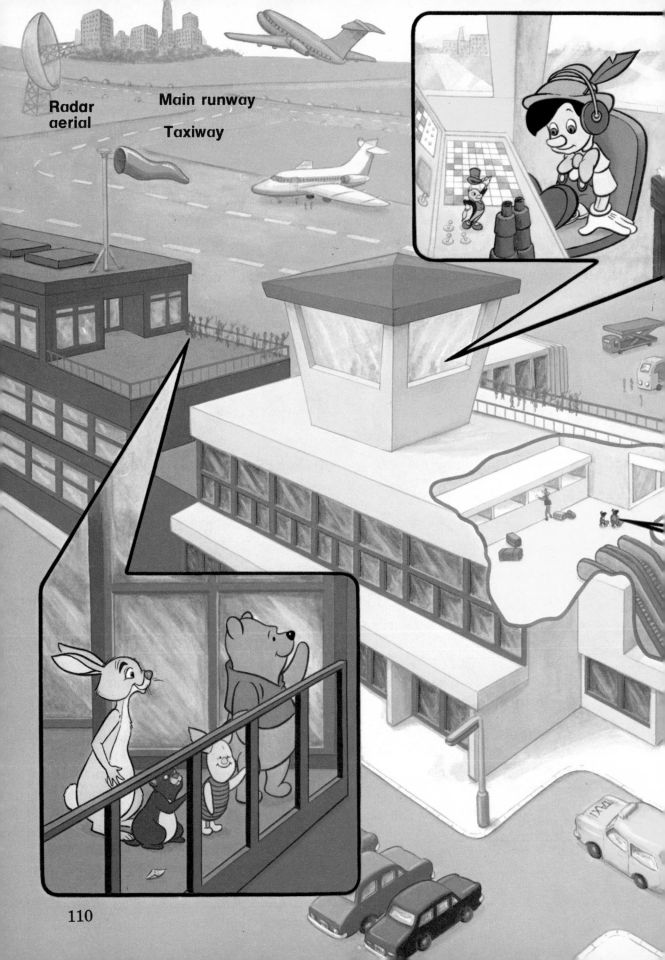

Radar
aerial

Main runway

Taxiway

An airport is a most exciting place to be, whether you are traveling yourself, or seeing someone off. It is a hive of activity. In the great international airports planes take off and land every minute or so. Many of these planes are jets carrying 400 passengers—you can imagine how hard the airport staff have to work to look after them all.

As well as the staff you see, there are many others that you don't. They include the traffic control officers in the control tower, who direct the planes in and out of the airport. There are the weather men, who keep an eye on the weather. In large hangars away from the main terminal building, maintenance engineers are servicing some of the planes; workers are loading and unloading cargo planes.

Apron

Airliner

At the Airport

The Terminal Building

The terminal building is the main passenger-handling area at the airport. It is carefully laid out so that passengers can pass through it as speedily as possible. If the passengers are delayed, it has facilities to keep them comfortable until the delays are over. It also

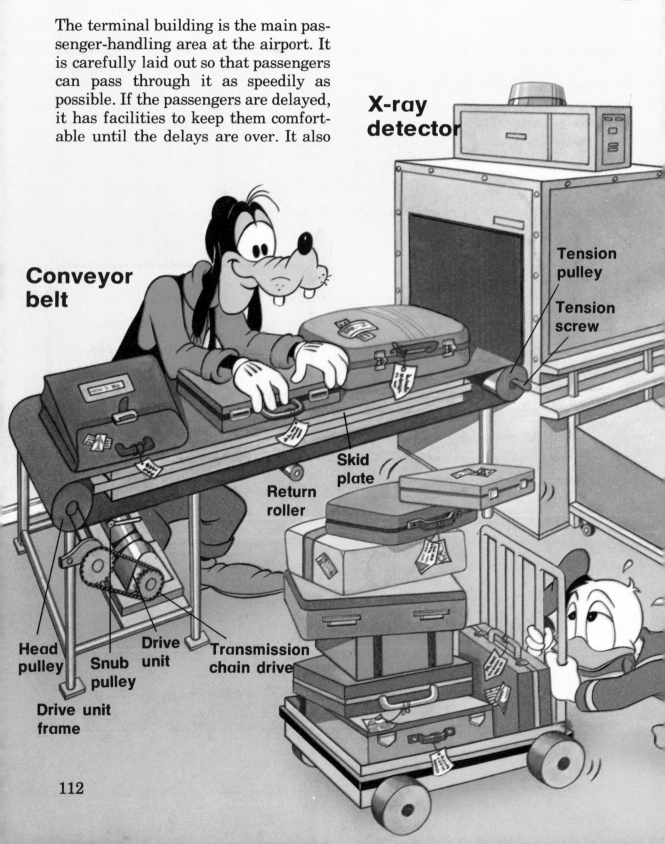

X-ray detector

Conveyor belt

Tension pulley

Tension screw

Skid plate

Return roller

Head pulley

Snub pulley

Drive unit

Transmission chain drive

Drive unit frame

has restaurants, bars, shops, banks and desks from which they can call hotels, buy theater tickets and hire cars.

If you are going to the airport to catch a plane yourself, the first thing you do when you arrive there is to check in. You go to the check-in counter of the airline on which you

have a reservation. The clerk checks your ticket, issues you a boarding card and weighs your luggage. On most overseas flights you are allowed to carry up to a certain weight. If your luggage weighs more than the limit, you have to pay extra for the excess weight. The clerk labels your luggage with your flight number and your destination and puts it on a conveyor belt which takes it to a luggage room. There it is sorted and eventually put on carriers which take it out to the airliner on which you will be traveling.

Before the luggage goes out of the room, it is passed through an X-ray machine. The reason for this is that some people may try to smuggle bombs and guns aboard the plane. This could be very dangerous for all the passengers and crew. If heavy metal objects are present in the luggage, the X-ray machine will find them with its invisible rays. Similarly, you and your hand luggage are scanned by an X-ray detector before you are allowed into the departure lounge, from where you will board your plane. Before that, if you are going to another country, you have to pass through immigration control, where your passport is checked and stamped.

In the departure lounge at an international airport there is usually a "duty-free" shop. There you can buy goods without paying import duty – a kind of tax. Without duty on them, goods such as cameras, watches, perfume, wines and spirits are very much cheaper – but don't buy too much! The airport to which you are traveling will only allow you to take in a certain amount of duty-free goods. If you want to take more, you will have to pay the usual duty.

All Aboard

While you and your fellow passengers are waiting in the departure lounge for your flight to be called, the plane on

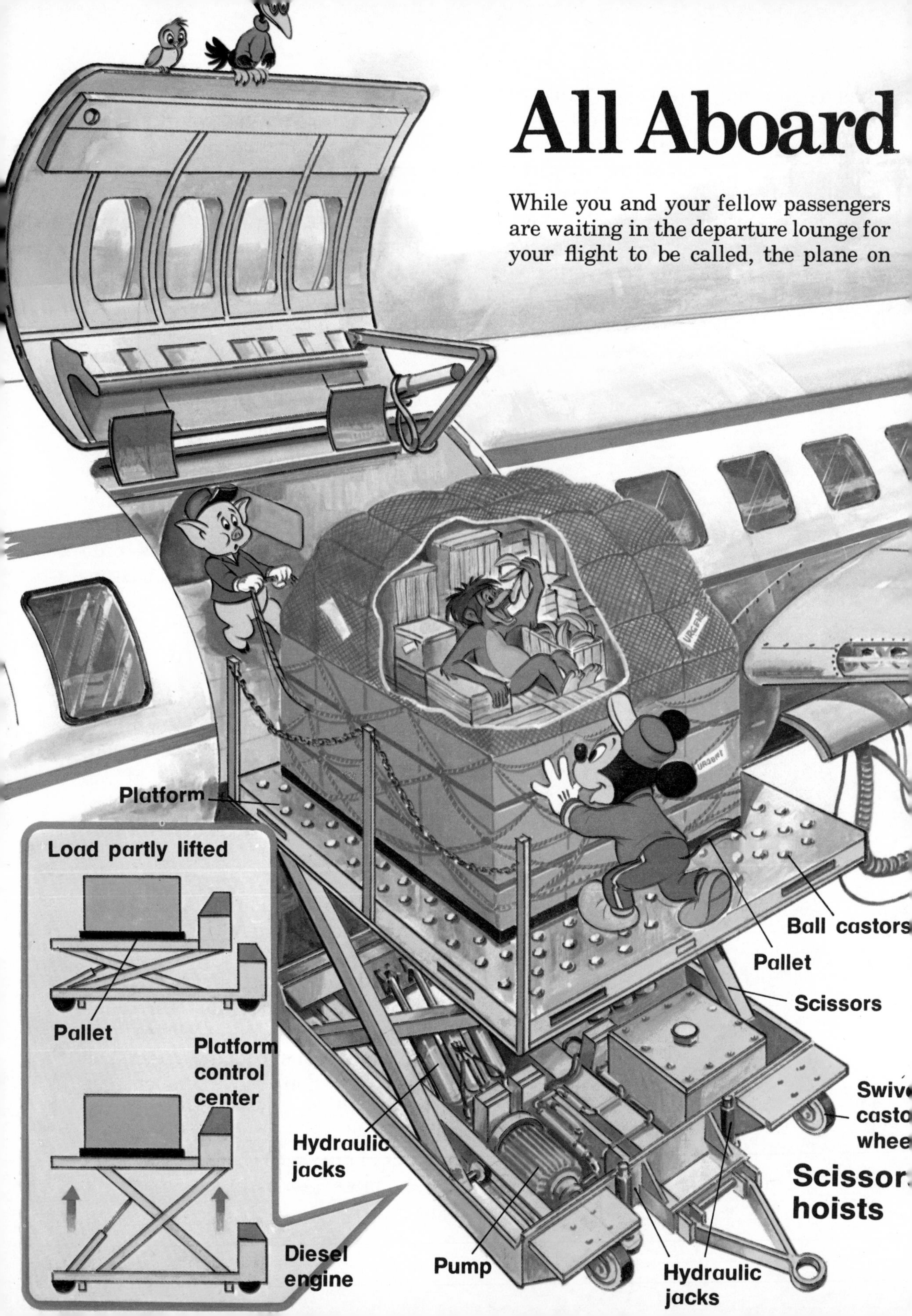

Platform

Ball castors

Pallet

Scissors

Swivel castor wheel

Scissors hoists

Load partly lifted

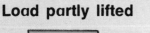

Pallet

Platform control center

Hydraulic jacks

Diesel engine

Pump

Hydraulic jacks

which you will be traveling is parked on the "apron" outside, and airport staff are preparing it for your flight.

The refueling team drives up in a fuel tanker, and pumps fuel through a hose into each of the plane's fuel tanks in

Fuel tanker

Refueling hose

turn. Often the tanks are housed in the wings. The fuel jet planes use is really a form of kerosene. They burn their fuel so quickly that their tanks have to be very large. The big Boeing-747 "jumbo" jet which flies across the Atlantic has seven tanks which hold a total of up to 40,000 gallons (190,000 liters) of fuel.

While refueling is going on, maintenance engineers may be checking the many instruments and control systems the plane has and putting right any minor problems. If they find anything seriously wrong, the plane is withdrawn from service and a different one put in its place.

At the same time, the passengers' luggage is being loaded, together with any other cargo that is being carried.

The caterer's truck delivers fresh supplies of food and drink, which the passengers will be served during their flight. A so-called scissors hoist is often used for loading. The load is placed on a pallet on the platform of the hoist at ground level. Then the platform is raised by hydraulic action. Powerful hydraulic jacks, which work by liquid pressure, extend the "scissors" beneath the platform, thus raising it. Liquid is pumped into the jacks from a pump driven by a diesel engine.

When it is your turn to board the plane, you may simply walk to where the plane is parked, or you may be carried there by traveling walkways or in huge mobile lounges. A smiling stewardess shows you to your seat. Soon it will be time to take off.

Upper lounge

Spiral
staircase

Main passenger
deck

Boeing 747 jumbo jet

Up and Away

Hinged
nose cone

Loading ramp

Take-off is one of the most exciting
parts of the whole plane journey. Even
the plane seems to shake with excite-
ment. A lighted panel comes on asking
you to fasten your seat belt. The cabin
door is closed, and the flight captain
welcomes you aboard.

He then starts the engines of the
plane and carries out the pre-flight
instrument checks to make sure everything is working properly. He does this
with his copilot and navigator. If the
flight will go over water, the steward-
esses show you how to strap on the
lifejackets provided under the seat.

When all checks have been com-
pleted, the pilot asks the control tower
for permission to take off. The traffic

controllers give him permission, and tell him to proceed along the taxiways to the beginning of the runway. With engines whining, the plane begins to move. It pauses, at the end of the runway, and the pilot throttles the engine to full power, but keeps the brakes on.

The whole plane shudders as the power increases and the engines scream. Suddenly the pilot releases the brakes and the plane hurtles down the runway at ever-increasing speed. In no time at all you are airborne. You hear a click as the landing gear folds up, or retracts, into the fuselage. Soon you have gone through the clouds and the plane stops climbing because it has reached its cruising height. For most airliners, this is up to about 30,000 ft (9,000 meters). The supersonic airliner Concorde, however, cruises twice as high! It also flies over twice as fast as most airliners, which cruise at about 600 mph (950 km/h).

If you fly in a Boeing 747 "jumbo jet," you can do something you can't do in other airliners. You can go upstairs! The 747 stands out from other airliners by having a bulbous front fuselage. There it has not one deck level, but two. At the front the upper deck forms the flight deck. At the rear it forms a lounge for the passengers.

The 747 is not only a passenger aircraft, it can also be adapted to carry freight, or cargo. As with many cargo carriers, the cargo is loaded through the front of the craft. The nose of the fuselage is hinged. The cargo plane shown here is being used to carry cars.

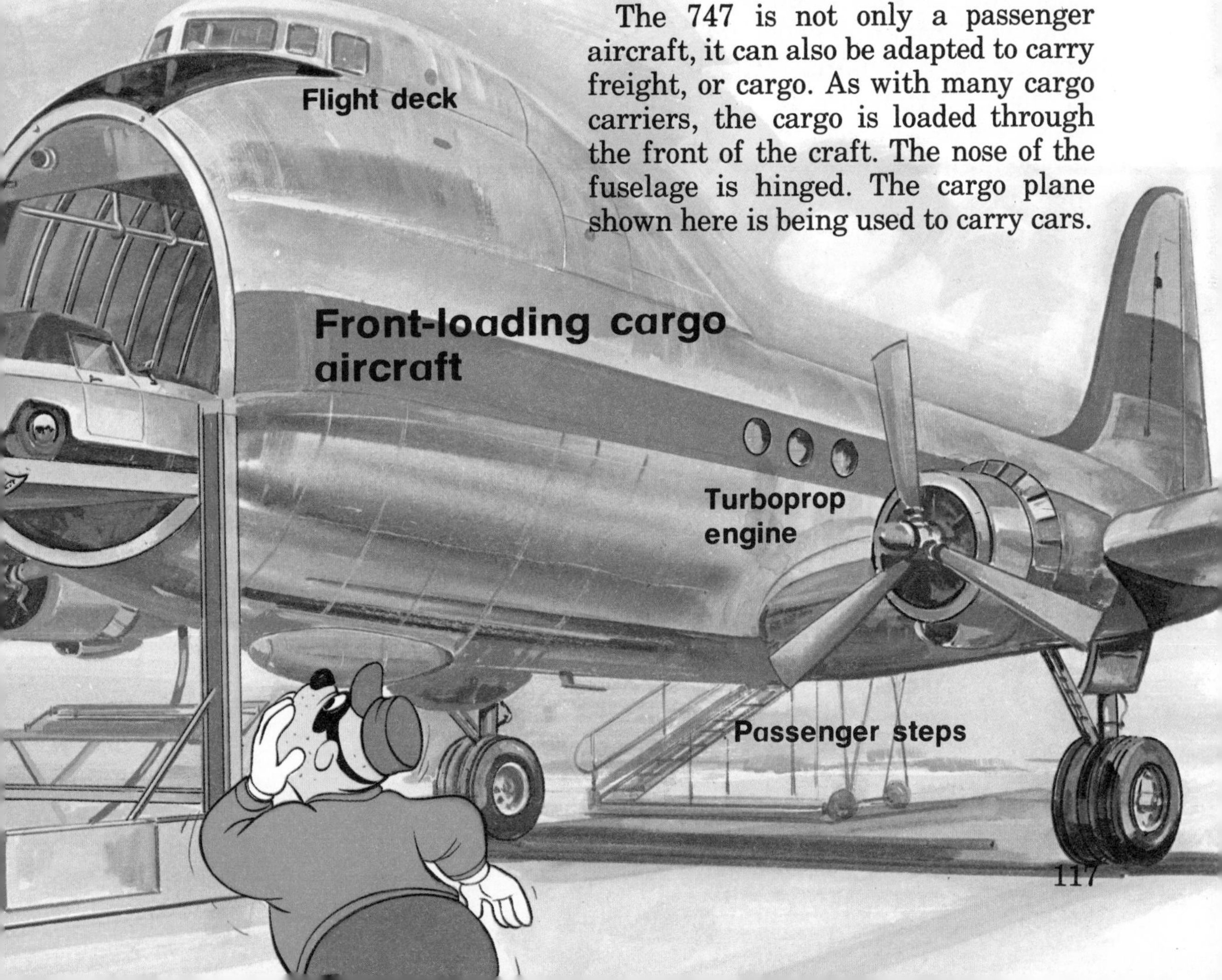

Flight deck

Front-loading cargo aircraft

Turboprop engine

Passenger steps

117

Flight Control

Some of the most important people at the airport are the flight, or air traffic controllers. They work in a high control tower from which they have a good view of the runways and taxiways. It is their job to make sure that the planes take off and land safely.

The controllers use all kinds of electronic communications to contact the pilots and their planes. They talk to them by radio, and pinpoint where they are by radar. Radar tells them the exact whereabouts of the planes in the sky. Knowing this, they can instruct pilots how best to approach the runway and when it is safe to do so.

The word radar is short for "radio detecting and ranging." Radar is a marvelous invention. It uses radio waves to detect objects in the sky and tell how far away the objects are and in which direction.

The three main parts of a radar set-up are a transmitter, an aerial and a receiver. The transmitter generates rapid pulses of radio waves, of a type known as microwaves. (Similar waves are used to cook food in microwave ovens.) The microwaves are fed to the aerial and sent out into the sky. When they hit something, such as an aircraft, they are reflected. The aerial picks up the reflection, or "echo," and feeds it to the receiver. The receiver has a screen very much like a television screen. When it receives an echo, a spot of light appears on the screen.

In order to get a complete picture of what is in the sky, radars use rotating aerials, or scanners, and the flight

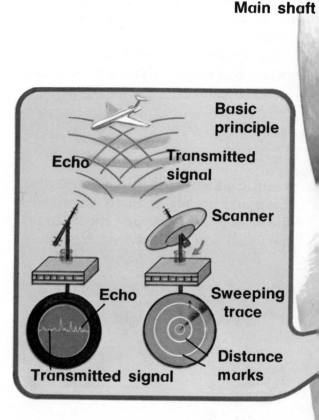

Main shaft

Basic principle

Echo

Transmitted signal

Scanner

Echo

Sweeping trace

Transmitted signal

Distance marks

controllers can tell from the position of the spot on the receiving screen in which direction the object that caused it lies. They can also tell how far away the object is.

In practice the flight controllers know which aircraft are entering or leaving the area. They can give information—for example, the latest weather and visibility reports.

Radar scanner

Solenoid

Antenna

Reflector

Scanner drive gear

Wave guide

Scanner drive motor

Generator

Radar screen

119

The Weather Station

There is a weather station at or near most airports. This is necessary so that pilots and flight controllers can know exactly what the weather conditions will be at any time. If a pilot knows that fog is likely to come down at one airport, he can make for another where fog is not expected.

Two very important things a pilot must know before he takes off or lands are the speed and direction of the wind. For safety, planes should always take-off and land into the wind, that is, with the wind blowing directly at them. A common method of indicating wind direction is with a so-called wind sock. This is a tube made out of fabric tied to a tall pole. It stands out like a flag when the wind blows.

The weather center has a more accurate way of measuring wind direction and speed. It uses a wind vane and anemometer. The anemometer has a number of cups mounted on a spindle which catch the wind and spin around. The harder the wind blows, the faster the cups spin. The wind speed is indicated on a dial. The wind direction is shown on another dial, linked to the wind vane.

The wind vane and anemometer at the weather center record the wind conditions close to the ground. Things might be different higher up, so the weather men release balloons into the air and then follow their path with a theodolite, a special kind of telescope. In some cases they may send up radiosondes. These are balloons carrying weather instruments. They also carry a radar reflector, so that they can be traced by radar after they have drifted out of visible range.

The weather men also measure such things as air temperature, air pressure, rainfall and humidity – the amount of moisture in the air. They measure the temperature with thermometers; the air pressure with barometers; the humidity with hygrometers; and the amount of rainfall with a rain gauge.

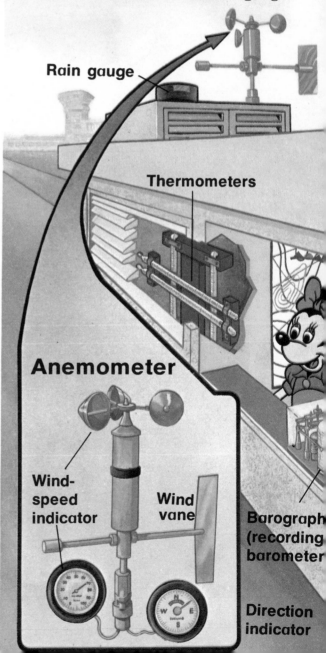

Rain gauge

Thermometers

Anemometer

Wind-speed indicator

Wind vane

Barograph (recording barometer)

Direction indicator

From their own readings and those from other weather stations, they construct a weather map, or synoptic chart. This shows the current weather pattern. From all this information they make their forecast.

Wind sock

Radar aerial

Weather map

Radiosonde balloon

Radar reflector

Theodolite

Instrument package

Instrument Flying

A pilot has many instruments in the cockpit to help him fly safely. The picture shows the instruments on the flight deck of the supersonic airliner Concorde. Flight instruments give the pilot information about the plane's speed and height, and the direction in which it is flying.

The main flight instruments include the air-speed indicator, which is the plane's "speedometer." It gives the speed of the plane through the air. The altimeter is another essential instrument, which tells the pilot how high he is. Some altimeters work by air pressure; others by radar.

The third main flight instrument is the compass, which tells the pilot in which direction the plane is heading.

A fourth important flight instrument is the artificial horizon. By looking at it the pilot always knows what his attitude is in the air. The same instrument also tells him whether he is climbing or diving.

The turn-and-bank indicator helps the pilot turn the plane correctly. The rate-of-climb indicator tells him how fast he is climbing or descending. Direction finders help him steer a correct course. An instrument landing system guides him on to the correct glide path for landing. During a long flight, the pilot may switch over to automatic pilot. This relies on the instruments to keep the plane on course.

Emergency Services

Clang, clang, clang go the alarm bells. Today everything is going wrong. The hat shop is on fire, the bank is being robbed; and Johnny has his head stuck between the railings. The telephone operator at the switchboard receives emergency calls from the frantic shopowner, bank manager and mother and switches them through at once to the fire department, police and ambulance drivers. Within seconds help in one form or another is on the way to put out the fire, apprehend the criminal and extract Johnny from the railings.

In the cities, where so many people live and where so much can go wrong, firemen, police, ambulance drivers and hospital workers are always ready at a moment's notice to offer assistance to those in trouble. In an emergency, run to a telephone booth and dial the emergency number displayed there.

125

Fire! Fire!

The firemen at the fire station spend a great deal of their time waiting around. They never know when they are going to be needed in a hurry, and so they are always prepared for quick action. Every day they test their equipment, examine their hoses, and make sure that their fire engine is filled with fuel and oil and starts easily. They regularly carry out firefighting practice, for as we all know "practice makes perfect."

Eventually the fire alarm bell rings and then they move swiftly into action. In many stations they slide down a pole from their quarters on the upper floor to the ground floor where the fire engine is. Each man knows exactly what he has to do. The driver starts up the engine; others bring the breathing apparatus, fireproof suits and cutting equipment.

The breathing apparatus will be required if the firemen have to go inside a smoke-filled house to rescue anyone. Asbestos suits will be needed to get close to very hot fires. Asbestos is a cloth made from rock fibers and is therefore heatproof. Cutting equipment is used when people are trapped in crashed vehicles, for example. It usually consists of a cutting torch and cylinders of the two gases oxygen and acetylene. These gases burn together in the oxyacetylene torch with a very hot flame that will cut through metal.

There are various kinds of fire engines, which are all equipped with powerful pumps, long lengths of hoses, flashing lights, bells or sirens and seats for the firefighting crew. They may have one of several kinds of body. The

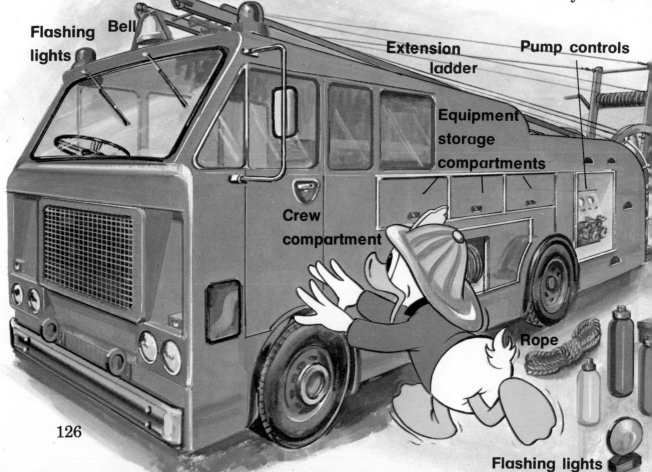

Flashing lights

Bell

Extension ladder

Pump controls

Equipment storage compartments

Crew compartment

Rope

Flashing lights

one shown here carries an extension ladder, which is mounted at the bottom on large wheels. These enable the ladder to be easily rolled into position. It is used to rescue people trapped on the upper floors of buildings or as a tower from which to direct water on to the flames.

Water is not always used for fire-fighting, however. It is of no use with oil and gasoline fires, because oil and gas float on water. It is dangerous to use water on electrical fires, because water conducts electricity. With these kinds of fires, firemen have to use such things as foam and carbon dioxide. These substances work by smothering the flames—preventing the oxygen in the air from reaching them. Without oxygen nothing can burn. Airport fire engines, or crash tenders as they are usually called, nearly always use foam for fire fighting because of the large amounts of fuel aircraft carry. The foam is delivered from a foam boom, or nozzle, on the roof of the driver's cab.

Sliding pole

Alarm bell

Fireproof suit

tting uipment

Axe

Saw

Breathing apparatus

On the Scene

When the fire engine arrives at the scene of the fire, the crew attach hoses between the pump and the nearest fire hydrants, which feed in water from the main. The pumps force water through other hoses which the firemen point at

Hose nozzle

Cage

Ladder

Mask

Air/oxygen cylinder

Powder

Release valve

Portable extinguisher

Discharge hose

the flames. These hoses end in metal nozzles, which make the water shoot out a long way with great force. Modern fire engines can pump out water at the rate of more than 1,000 gallons (4,500 liters) a minute!

To reach the top floors of buildings firemen use their extension ladders, or hydraulic lift platforms like that shown in the picture. It is similar to the type maintenance engineers use to repair street lights. When traveling,

the booms are folded flat. In use, a fireman climbs into the cage, and then hydraulic jacks force the booms to rise. The whole boom assembly is rotated on a turntable until the fireman is in the best position. A hose attached to the boom carries water to a movable nozzle mounted on the cage.

With all the hats burning in this store, there is a lot of smoke, and one of the firemen has decided to put on breathing apparatus before he goes inside with a portable fire extinguisher. The breathing apparatus consists of a mask supplied with oxygen or compressed air from a cylinder strapped on the back. The mask fits tightly over the face and enables the fireman to breathe while surrounded by smoke.

The portable extinguisher the fireman is carrying is called a dry extinguisher, because it delivers powder and gas. When the safety clip is out and the release valve is open, compressed carbon dioxide gas forces the powder up the dip tube and out through the discharge hose. The powder forms a crust on the burning material. This, together with the carbon dioxide, helps to keep out the air and therefore extinguish the fire.

There are several other kinds of fire extinguishers. Some contain only carbon dioxide. Some spray carbon tetrachloride, which is a liquid once widely used for dry cleaning clothes. This type is very good for electrical fires. Soda-acid extinguishers contain a mixture of sulphuric acid and a solution of bicarbonate of soda. When the two are mixed, carbon dioxide gas is produced which forces the solution out through a hose.

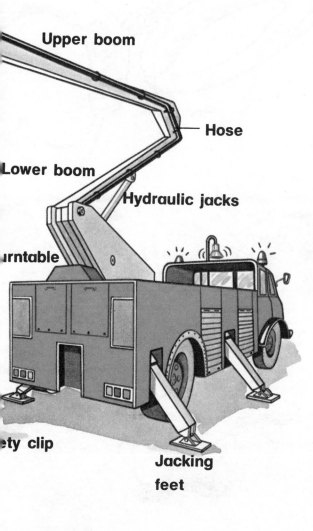

Upper boom

Hose

Lower boom

Hydraulic jacks

urntable

ety clip

Jacking feet

rbon dioxide

Dip tube

In the Police Station

If you remember, on page 125 you saw the bank being robbed. As the burglar entered the bank, he set off an alarm in the police station. It is just one of many connected to businesses and shops in the surrounding district. The policemen rushed to the bank and caught the burglar "red-handed." They have handcuffed him and brought him back to the police station for questioning.

When the police question someone, they don't always get truthful answers! Suspects also often give a false name. To help them identify their suspect, they take his fingerprints, because a person's fingerprints are unique. No other person has fingerprints like them, and they remain unchanged throughout life.

To take fingerprints, the tip of each finger in turn is first pressed on an ink pad and then on white paper. The fingerprints show up clearly as a black and white pattern because the skin on the fingertips is made up of a series of tiny ridges. The ridges form patterns

Key

Handcuffs

Line-up

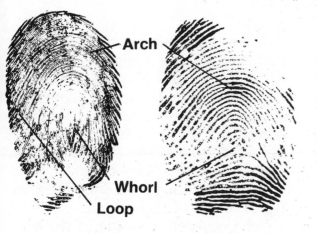

Arch

Whorl

Loop

called arches, loops (like a horseshoe) and whorls (like a circle). After the prints have been taken, they are photographed and compared with other prints in a central file. This comparison is now usually done with the help of computers.

Sometimes the police arrive too late at the scene of a crime and the person who committed it has disappeared, but they may be lucky to find a witness— someone who saw the person. When they have a suspect, they call the witness to a line-up. They stand their suspect in a line with several other people of similar appearance taken from the street, and the witness picks out the person he thinks he saw. If he chooses the suspect, then this is used as evidence in court.

A country police station may be very small, sometimes little more than a room in the policeman's house, but a central police station can be as big as a city block. It will have cells to keep people locked up; a desk where the public can give information and make inquiries; interview rooms; and numerous offices in which policemen carry out all the background work necessary in their fight against crime.

Fingerprinting

Alarm console

On Patrol

One of the main jobs of the police is to patrol the streets. This is usually done by policemen in uniform.

The police do not just wander idly arcund. They always keep their eyes open for signs of burglary, for wanted people and for stolen cars. They are also on hand to control traffic and to give advice. They are also equipped with walkie-talkie radios.

Policemen not only patrol their beat on foot, but also on wheels – on motorcycles and in cars. Many of these vehicles have specially tuned engines to give them extra speed, and they are equipped with powerful walkie-talkie radios. They also have flashing lights and sirens, which they switch on in an emergency to clear a path through the traffic ahead of them.

Driving too fast is one of the commonest offenses on the roads. On most roads these days there is a speed limit,

Crystals

Breathalizer kit

Breathalizer bag

Runaway lawn mower

Portable two-way radio

Radar gu

which varies from place to place and from country to country.

Traffic cops can check your speed by following behind you. They can also check it by radar. The radar apparatus sends out signals, which are reflected back by your car. The signals are altered according to your speed, which shows up on a meter attached to the apparatus. Radar hand "guns" are now also being used to check car speeds.

Another serious traffic offense is driving under the influence of alcohol.

When a driver has drunk too much alcohol, his reflexes – the way he reacts to things – are slowed down. This can and does cause many accidents. Therefore, when an accident has occurred, the police may ask the driver to take a breathalizer test. Often this is done by the driver blowing into a bag in which there are certain crystals. The way the crystals change color gives an indication of how much alcohol the driver has been drinking.

Flashing light

Transparent casing

Bulb

Revolving reflector

Counterweight

Motor

Burglars

Two-way radio

Digital speed indicator

Test buttons

Trigger

Police car

133

The Emergency Room

Accidents happen every day – in traffic, at home, at work or at play. When accidents do happen, the people who are hurt are taken to the hospital emergency room. There doctors and nurses are on duty all through day and night.

A doctor can often tell what is the matter with you just by looking, but to get more information he may examine you with simple instruments. Perhaps his "best friend" is his stethoscope.

The stethoscope consists of two earpieces and a chestpiece connected by rubber tubing. The chestpiece is held against the patient's chest and picks up body sounds. These are then carried by tubing to the earpieces. The earpieces fit snugly into the ears and help block out outside noises. The chestpiece is made up of two parts – a cone, or bell, and a flatter cup, or diaphragm. The cone picks up low sounds best; the diaphragm, high sounds.

Your body temperature may also tell the doctor something about your health. The normal body temperature is 98.4 F. The doctor takes your temperature with a clinical thermometer. This is not like an ordinary thermometer. This is filled with mercury and has a constriction in the tube.

Most ordinary thermometers are filled with colored alcohol and have no constriction. If such a thermometer were used to take the temperature, the column of liquid would start to fall as soon as it was taken from the patient's mouth and the doctor could never get an accurate reading. Putting a constriction in the thermometer tube prevents the mercury from falling back

after the thermometer has been removed from the mouth.

The doctor may also take your blood

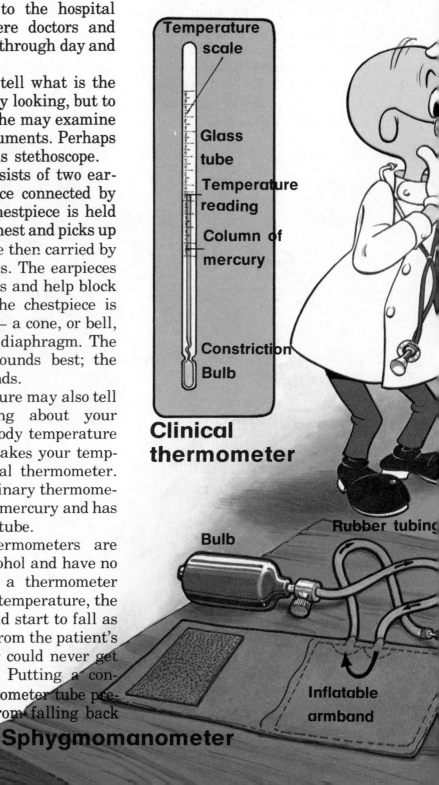

Temperature scale

Glass tube

Temperature reading

Column of mercury

Constriction

Bulb

Clinical thermometer

Rubber tubing

Bulb

Inflatable armband

Sphygmomanometer

pressure. He does this with a sphyg-momanometer. This consists of an inflatable armband (cuff) connected to a tube of mercury. The armband is wrapped around the arm just above the elbow, and air is pumped into it by pressing a bulb. The air pressure in the armband pushes up the column of mercury along a scale. Eventually the pressure is so high that it closes up the artery carrying blood in the arm. The reading on the scale then gives the blood pressure.

Scale

Mercury

Cone

Diaphragm

Earpieces

Stethoscope

Seeing Through You

Another important section of the hospital is the X-ray department. By studying photographs of your body taken with X-rays, doctors can find out much about what is happening inside you.

X-rays are invisible rays which can pass right through your body. They also affect photographic film, as light

Fluorescent screen

Film holder

X-ray scanner

Lead-glass window

Control console

X-ray tube under tilting examination table

Glass bulb

does. In the hospital technicians called radiographers take photographs with X-rays after they have passed through your body. The X-rays pass more easily through the fleshy parts of the body than through the bones and organs,

and on the X-ray photographs the bones and organs show up. Doctors can tell much from X-ray photographs. For example, they can tell if the bones are broken or if there are signs of lung disease such as tuberculosis.

Doctors also use X-rays to help them reset broken bones. They use an X-ray machine called a fluoroscope. This has a fluorescent screen which glows when X-rays strike it. A doctor can see from the picture on the screen the best way of positioning the broken bones so that they set well.

The latest X-ray machine produces photographs of a thin "slice" of the body. It is known as an X-ray scanner. It views the "slice" from many angles, and a detector beneath the body records the X-rays passing through each time. All the information is fed into a computer, which then displays an X-ray picture of the "slice" on a screen. Pictures taken in this way show up very great detail.

The X-rays themselves are produced in a vacuum tube (one from which all the air has been removed). In the tube a cathode (negative electrode) gives off electrons when it is heated by electricity. The electrons travel to the anode (positive electrode), which takes the form of a rotating disc, or target. As the electrons strike the target, X-rays are given off. The target is rotated to keep it cool.

The X-rays pass out of the tube through a "window." The rest of the tube is enclosed in lead, which prevents X-rays escaping through it. Such lead shielding is needed to protect the radiographers. In small doses X-rays are harmless, but in large doses they can be harmful.

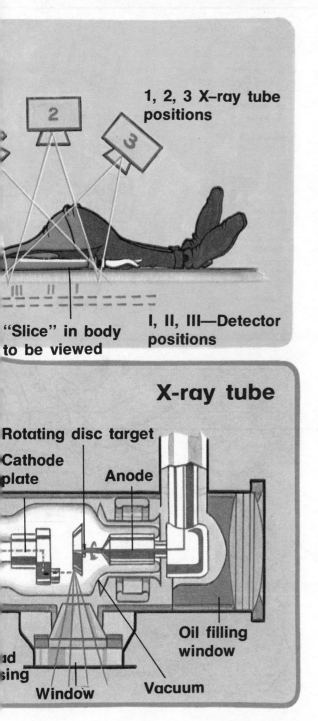

1, 2, 3 X-ray tube positions

"Slice" in body to be viewed

I, II, III—Detector positions

X-ray tube

Rotating disc target

Cathode plate

Anode

Oil filling window

Window

Vacuum

That's Entertain-ment

For most of the day the city is a frantic place of business and work, travel and sight-seeing, but when the business day is coming to an end, a new business world is coming to life – the world of show business – and there's no business like show business, so they say.

Actors and artists start arriving at the theaters and getting dressed and made-up ready for the evening shows. Lines start forming at the movies, waiting for the last performance of the latest hit film release. Bowling alleys echo with the clatter of tumbling pins. Amusement arcades resound to the clink of coins in the slot machines and noisy music, tempting you inside to spend your money.

139

At the Movies

Going to the movies to see films has been a popular form of entertainment since the beginning of the century.

At the movie theater you see what appear to be moving pictures, but actually the pictures thrown, or projected on to the screen, are not moving. If they were, all you would see would be a blur. What actually happens is that a series of still pictures are projected on to the screen, one after the other in quick succession. Between them the screen is blank, but the eye holds on to the image of each picture as the next comes into view and doesn't see any "gap" between them. (This is called the persistence of vision.) Any objects that were moving in the original scene are shown in a slightly different position from picture to picture. As the eye joins the pictures together, the objects appear to move.

The pictures are taken on a continuous ribbon of film, usually 35 millimeters wide, wound on a spool. They are thrown on to the screen at a rate of 24 frames (separate pictures) a second. The apparatus that "throws" them on to the screen is the projector. In the projector a bright light shines through the film, and a magnified image of the picture is thrown on to the distant screen by a lens. While the light shines through it, the film is held still. Then a rotating shutter blots out the light as the film moves on one frame.

In a movie projector the light is provided by an arc lamp, which is very brilliant. It consists of two carbon rods connected to a direct (one-way) current supply. When the rods are moved slightly apart, electricity "jumps" between them, forming a continuous electric spark called an arc. A curved mirror (condenser) behind the arc concentrates the arc light on the film.

Movie projector

Film spo[ol]

Clamp

Carbon rod

Arc lamp

Film

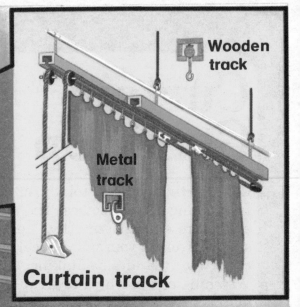

Curtain track

Wooden track

Metal track

Window

Screen

Projection lens

Film cans

The sounds that accompany the projected pictures are also recorded on the film in the form of a sound track at the side. Some sound tracks are optical – they use a photographic pattern on the film. Others are magnetic – they use a magnetic coating, like a tape recording. A sound "head" picks up signals from the sound track and feeds them to a set of loudspeakers either at the side of the screen or behind it. In each speaker the signals go through the voice coil, and make the cone vibrate. This causes the sounds.

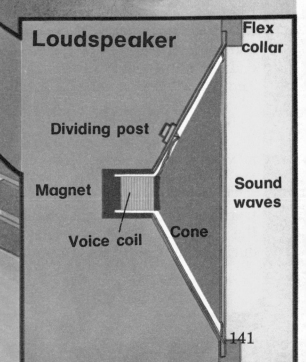

Loudspeaker

Flex collar

Dividing post

Magnet

Sound waves

Voice coil

Cone

141

Curtain Going Up

Going to the theater is totally different from going to the movies. The actors and actresses perform "live" on the stage in front of you, and you feel much closer to the drama taking place. Watching and listening to great actors and actresses in a great play is an unforgettable experience. They have a "presence" that captivates you. All kinds of dramatic works have their place in the theater: grim tragedies and lighthearted comedies, classical operas and modern musicals, ballets and pantomimes.

In the ordinary theater the audience sit in rows of seats in a horseshoe-shaped auditorium. The seats are arranged in tiers, each row getting higher the further it is away from the stage. In this way people at the rear can see over the heads of the people in front of them. Main floor seats are called orchestra seats. Many theaters and concert halls have seats on a second and a third level, called balconies. The highest level is called the gallery. Theater seats are usually upholstered to be comfortable. They fold up when not in use. This gives people room to move between the rows. Theater seats are also numbered.

The stage is usually set in a kind of frame, called the proscenium. Before the play starts and between scenes during the play, the proscenium is

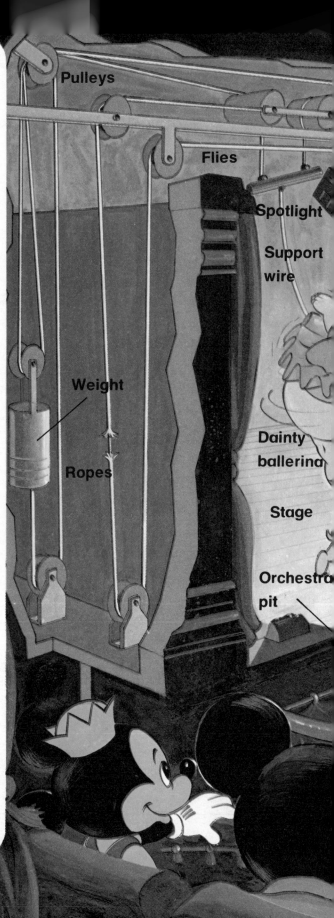

Pulleys

Flies

Spotlight

Support wire

Weight

Ropes

Dainty ballerina

Stage

Orchestra pit

Scenery

Flying harness

Footlights

Musicians

Balcony

Audience

Seats in tiers

covered by a curtain. This is drawn aside or lifted when the play begins. Some theaters do not have a proscenium, but have an open stage, around which the audience sits on three sides. Others have a completely circular stage, or arena, rather like the ancient Greek theaters.

In the ordinary theater the proscenium hides all the mechanical gadgets and lighting equipment needed to help the drama taking place on stage. This can include, as the picture shows, the ropes and pulleys needed to lift and move the "flying" performers in an aerial ballet. Each wears a harness wired to a traveling carriage. The rope and pulley system includes a heavy counterweight which makes it easier to lift the performer.

Fold-up seat

Behind the Scenes

A lot happens behind the scenes at the theater both before and during a performance. The actors and actresses have to dress up in their stage clothes and may have to change costumes several times to fit the varied moods and actions as the plot unfolds.

They have to put on make-up, too, which can take quite a long time. It is almost always necessary to wear make-up on stage because of the harsh lighting. Actors and actresses may use straight make-up or character make-up. They use straight make-up to emphasize their own features, while they use character make-up to change their appearance – to become a different character.

One of the commonest materials used for make-up is grease paint. It comes in tubes and sticks of every conceivable shade and color. It is used as a foundation color and for highlights. Pancake make-up is also used – it is applied by a wet sponge. Mascara for eyelashes and lipstick are always widely used – often for the actors as well as the actresses!

Strengthened eyebrows

Eye shadow

High light

Pulleys

Harness

Eye hollow

Nose shading

Dancer

Lip coloring

Cheek bones shading

Flying apparatus

Straight make-up

Make-up artist

Lighting plays an important part in the theater and several sets of lights are always used. Around the front of the stage, at stage level, are the footlights, which shed a soft light on to the stage. Brighter floodlights, usually arranged in groups, provide general lighting for the set, or scene on the stage. They are usually mounted in the

flies. This is a system of rails above the stage which is hidden from the audience. Also in the flies is the apparatus for operating the curtains and moving the scenery.

To highlight parts of the set or focus attention on one of the characters, spotlights are used. They may be mounted in the flies or at the front in the body of the theater. A lighting technician operates all the lights from a switchboard. He can use a dimmer switch to make the lights fade on and off gradually. The switch increases or decreases the resistance in the electrical circuits, making the current fall or rise.

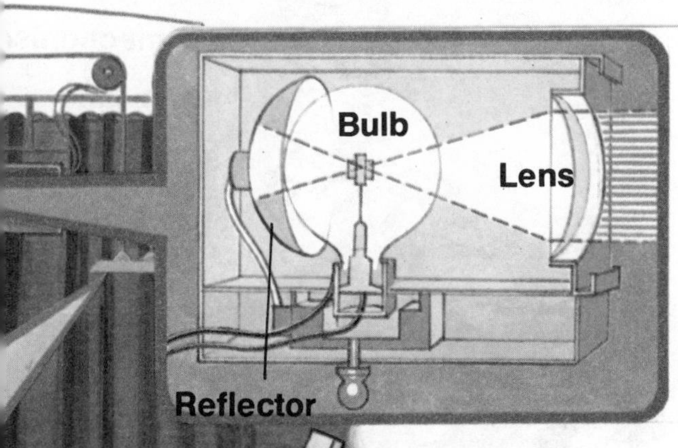

Bulb

Lens

Reflector

Spotlight

Scenery

Dimmer switch

age hands

Lighting technician

Actors

Fun Machines

Even if you have only a few coins in your pocket, you can still find places in the city to have fun. You can, for example, go into an amusement arcade. In the arcade are all kinds of pinball or slot machines on which you can try your luck or test your skill. On some machines you play simply for the fun of it. On others you may win some money or prizes.

One common machine is the fruit machine, or "one-armed bandit." It is so-called because it has an operating handle like an arm, and if you lose, you say it robbed you! To work the machine, you pull down the handle and this sets three reels spinning around. On the reels are pictures of different kinds of fruit. When the reels stop, they each display a fruit in the window. When certain combinations of fruit appear in the window – say, three apples – then you win a prize. A mechanism in the machine pays you out a number of coins. From time to time you may get a rare combination of fruits, and win the "jackpot." Then you can win a lot of money.

Another popular fun machine is the pinball machine. This is played with a metal ball on a sloping table. Dotted around the table are mushroom-shaped "bumper" units. To play the machine you propel a ball up the board with a plunger. As the ball rolls back down the board, it hits various bumper units. When it hits them you score points, the lamp inside lights up, and a coil device knocks the ball away. The bumper unit works by elec-

One-arme bandit

Reel mechanisr

Coin tube

Payout unit

Cash box

Lamp

Bumper ring

Bumper skirt

Control buttons

Solenoid

Solenoid switch contacts

tromagnetic coils, or solenoids. Your score is automatically added up as you play and displayed in a window.

A more recent addition to the amusement arcade is the video game, which uses a television-type screen. The players use their controls to move beams of electrons which make the picture on the screen. The screen is mounted horizontally and is viewed through a semi-silvered mirror, set at an angle. Behind the mirror is a panel painted with suitable scenery. With this arrangement the players see the video picture against a scenic background. A minicomputer is the brains behind the game, and also switches in appropriate sound effects to suit the action, for example, gunfire.

Video game

- Glass panels
- Angled semi-silvered mirror
- Scenery
- Coin selector
- Picture tube
- Score
- Operating handle
- Coin hopper

Pinball machine

- Metal ball
- Plunger

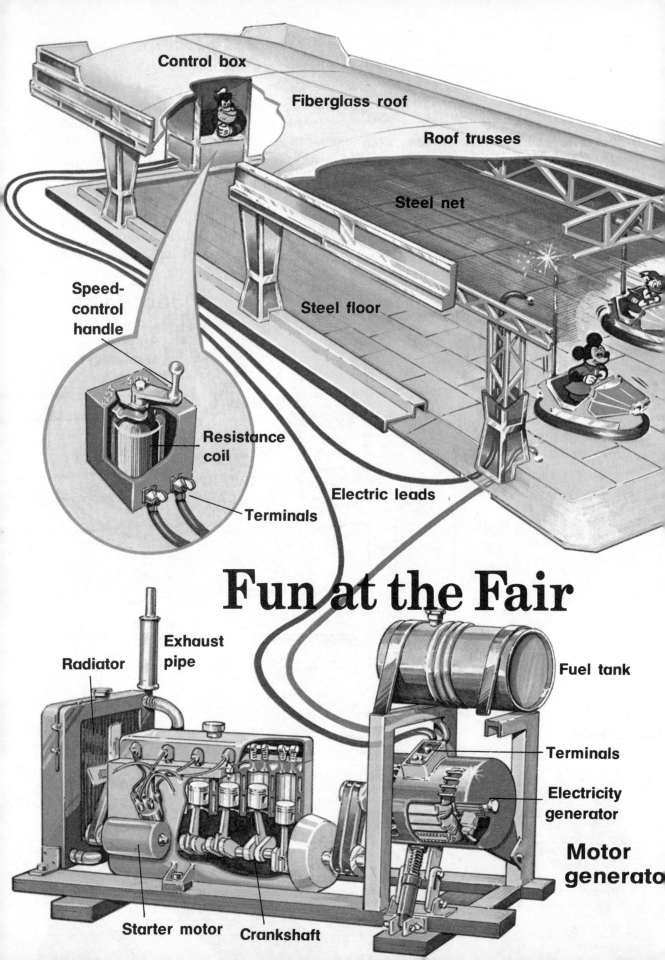

Control box

Fiberglass roof

Roof trusses

Steel net

Steel floor

Speed-control handle

Resistance coil

Terminals

Electric leads

Fun at the Fair

Radiator

Exhaust pipe

Fuel tank

Terminals

Electricity generator

Motor generato

Starter motor

Crankshaft

There are few among us, young or old, who can resist going to a carnival or fair, for at a fair there is something for everyone to do. You can ride on all kinds of whirling machines, from merry-go-rounds and "Ferris wheels" to ingenious switchbacks and flying

structure which has a floor of steel plates and a roof covered over with steel net. Electricity is produced by an engine-driven generator and fed to the structure. One lead goes to the steel floor, the other to the steel net. The dodgem car is driven by electric motor in the front wheel. It picks up electricity to drive the motor by making contact with the floor and the roof net. It makes contact with the floor through its back wheels, and with the net by a vertical arm, which has a sliding contact, or slipper, at the top. A pedal in the car operates a switch that turns the power to the motor on or off.

machines that twist and turn and rock and roll.

A firm favorite year after year is the "dodgems," which are small electric cars that you drive yourself. Perhaps a better name for them would be "hit 'ems," for the drivers are always bumping into each other!

The dodgem cars run in a special

Contact slipper

Aluminum tread plate

Dodgem car

Wire to motor

Steel wheel

Fiberglass body

Steering wheel

Rubber tire

Bevel gear

Drive motor

Rubber bumper

Pedal

On/Off switch

Flying High and Low

The picture shows one of the flying machines you can find at a modern fair. You whirl around at high speed in "planes" which you can make go up and down yourself. The planes are fixed to arms that extend from a central hub. The hub rests on a turntable and is spun around by a powerful drive motor underneath. Its speed is controlled by a variable resistance. This alters the electric current going to the drive motor from a generator like the one shown on the previous pages.

The arm carrying each plane is

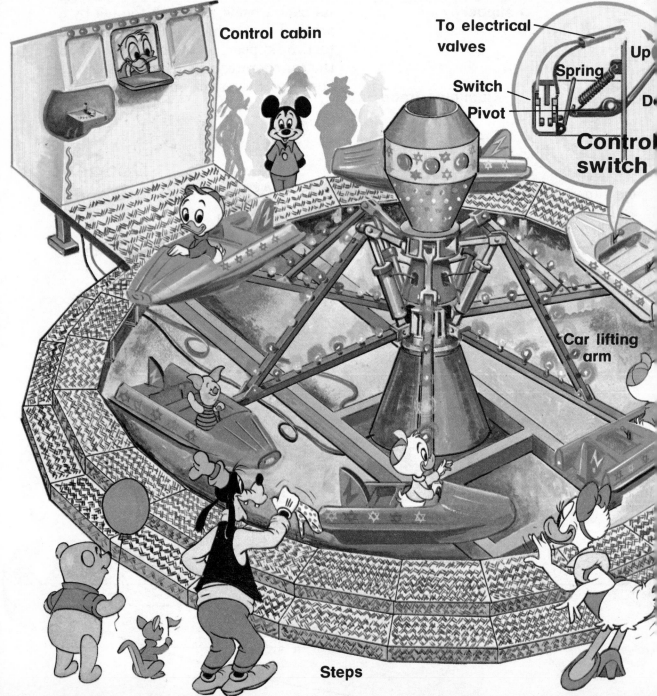

Control cabin

To electrical valves

Switch

Pivot

Spring

Up

D

Control switch

Car lifting arm

Steps

linked to the hub by pivoted joints and a hydraulic ram. This is a ram which works by liquid pressures. The arm is linked in such a way that it rises when the ram is pushed out. This happens when hydraulic fluid is forced into the ram by a pump and pushes against the piston inside. On the other hand, the arm carrying the plane drops when fluid is let out of the ram.

The movement of fluid into and out of the ram is controlled by electrically operated valves. These valves are worked in turn by the driver of the plane by moving the control switch in front of him. Each plane is linked separately to the hub, and so each driver can go up or down independently.

The fluid to work the ram is contained in a tank in the top of the hub unit. It is pumped in and out as the arms rise and fall.

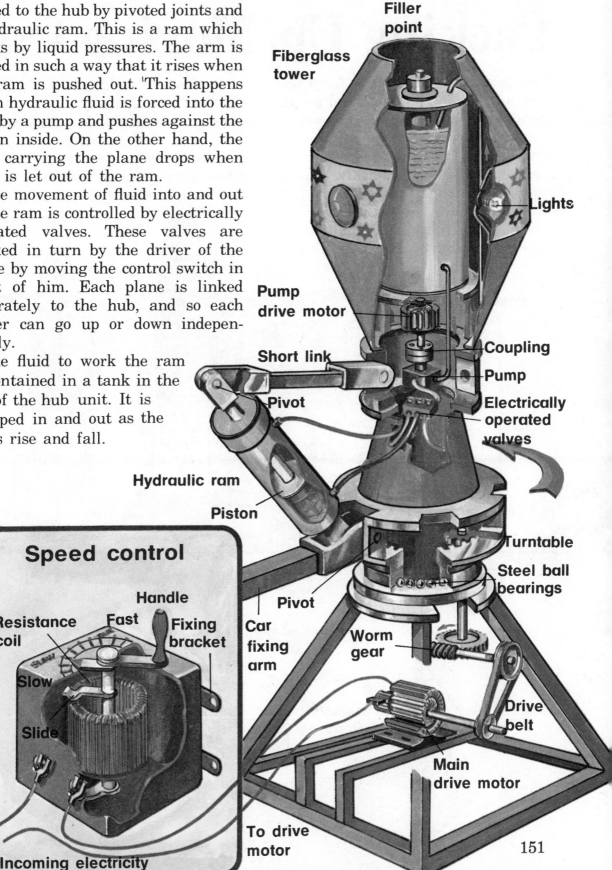

Filler point

Fiberglass tower

Lights

Pump drive motor

Coupling

Short link

Pump

Pivot

Electrically operated valves

Hydraulic ram

Piston

Turntable

Speed control

Pivot

Steel ball bearings

Handle

Resistance coil

Fast

Fixing bracket

Car fixing arm

Worm gear

Slow

Drive belt

Slide

Main drive motor

To drive motor

Incoming electricity

151

Packing Up, Moving On

Fairs are usually held only for a few days at a time, and fairground people spend a great deal of time traveling from place to place. Their equipment is therefore designed to be put together and taken apart very quickly. A good example is the flying machine just described (pages 150-151).

The whole machine is built on a heavy steel frame, or chassis. When the machine is working, the chassis is supported by four hydraulic rams. For moving, the chassis is made into a trailer by sliding pairs of wheels beneath the front and rear. It can then be towed by a heavy truck. The front-wheel unit is mounted on a slew ring,

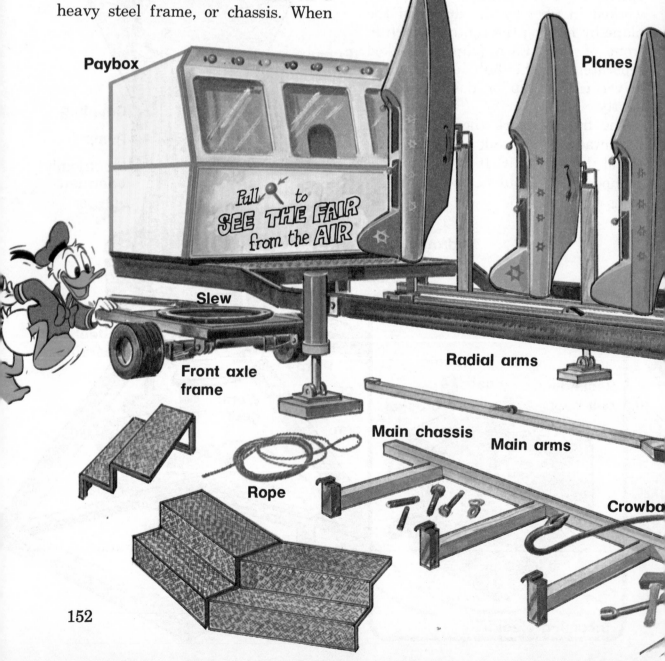

Paybox

Pull to SEE THE FAIR from the AIR

Planes

Slew

Front axle frame

Radial arms

Main chassis

Main arms

Rope

Crowba

or pivot, beneath the chassis so that it can be steered. A trailer board, with lights and direction indicators is hung at the rear.

The rest of the machine easily splits up into units which stack on the chassis. The plane bodies are stacked vertically and are fixed to supporting frames at the sides. The steps up from the ground are made so that they stack one upon the other. Fixing pins, lamps, tools and other loose items are stored in the paybox. As much equipment as possible is made of aluminum or fiberglass because these materials are light in weight.

It can take a day or more to dismantle and stack the flying machine. Then, perhaps after an overnight journey, the operating crew arrives at the site of the next fair and starts putting it all back together again!

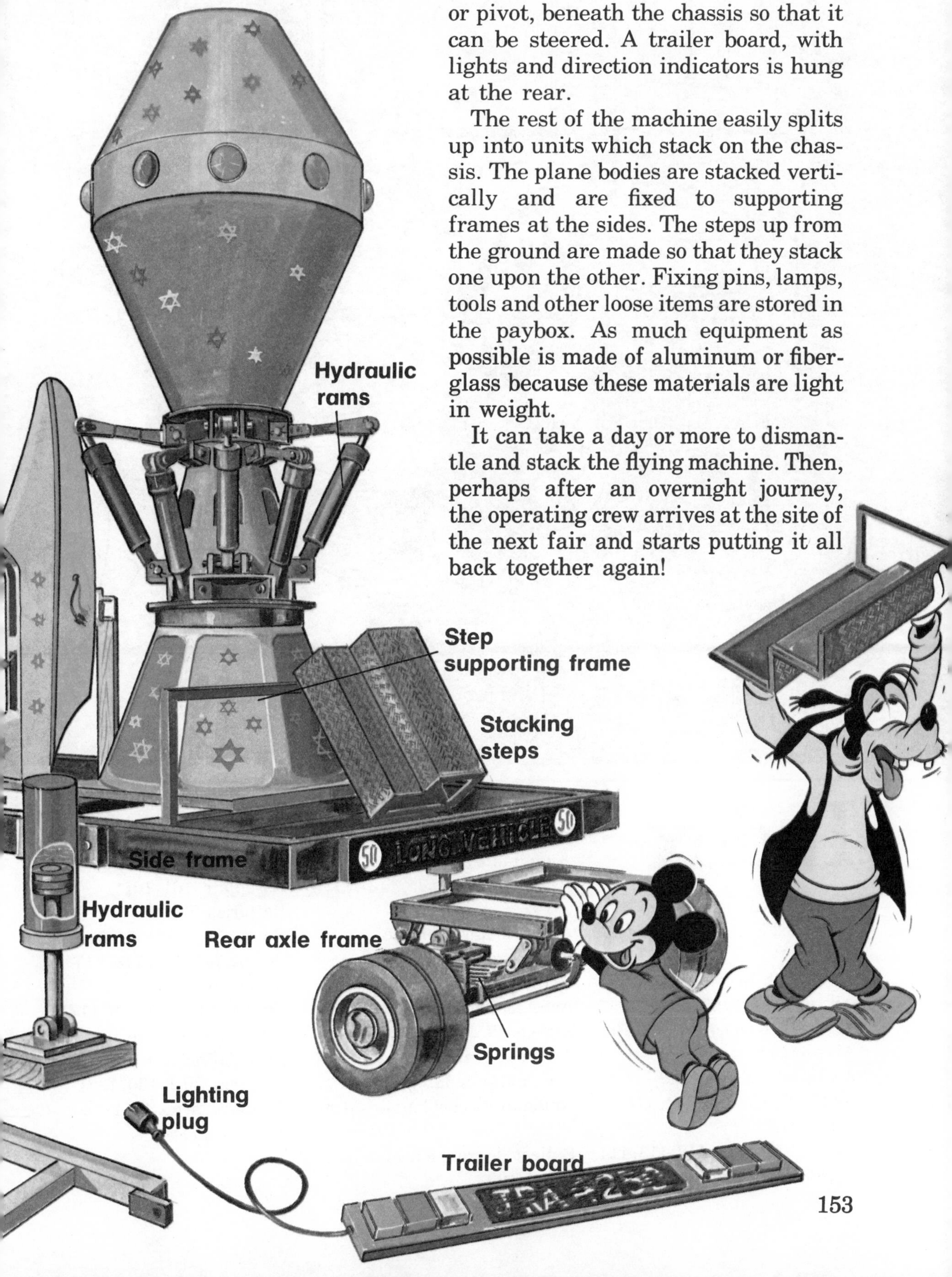

Hydraulic rams

Step supporting frame

Stacking steps

Side frame

Hydraulic rams

Rear axle frame

Springs

Lighting plug

Trailer board

153

Index